Using the Bible with All Ages Together

Donald L. Griggs
and Patricia R. Griggs

Series editor:
Wendy S.Robins

Bible Society

This publication by Bible Society (Publishing), Swindon, Wilts
ISBN 0 564 07152 8

Printed by Borough Press (Wiltshire) Limited

Contents

The Authors

Donald and Patricia Griggs have conducted numerous workshops for Christian educators in various parts of America. Together they have developed many resources which include books, pamphlets, filmstrips, cassettes, and other instructional aids.

Also by Donald Griggs in the *Using the Bible Series: In Teaching, With Audio-Visuals* and *For All Who Teach*.

Editor's Note

Throughout this book, we have decided to keep the American edition's usage of the terms "goals" and "objectives", as defined in chapter 1 on page 23. This may differ from British usage, which is often the reverse.

Preface to the American edition

Greetings to our colleagues in Christian education.

This book has taken us a long time to put together. We have been working at reaching people of various ages together in one class for about ten years now. We have sensed a tremendous value to this style of teaching. We sense that many others in churches across America have been discovering the values of involving mixed age groups in common learning experiences. If you share an interest in and commitment to planning for all ages learning together then we welcome you to the adventure of exploring ways to approach this style of teaching.

Perhaps you too have searched for resources to guide you in planning for intergenerational learning activities and have been frustrated, as we have, by not being able to find much that was helpful. We have had to create from scratch, adapt from other resources, and experiment with resources and activities to see what would work. Sometimes we were successful and other times we had to start over again to see if there was another way to make it work.

Many people have written and spoken to us about their experiences of teaching mixed age groups. And many have encouraged us to use our experiences and our publishing enterprise in order to pull together some resources that might be helpful to others who plan for generations learning together. So, we have taken the suggestions seriously and have responded to the encouragement to present in this book some basic principles, some planning suggestions, and some possible session plans.

From its beginnings Griggs Educational Service has been a family enterprise. We have three generations working together in various aspects of the enterprise. We can assure you that we have learned and grown a lot as a result of our struggles together as parents, grandparents, children and grandchildren in a common life, work and ministry. Each generation has its own gifts, its own insights, its own needs. A family, a community, a church is not whole unless the gifts, insights, and needs of all its members are brought together in a shared life of love and commitment.

We three generations of Griggs wish you the joy, excitement and sense of satisfaction that comes from having worked hard to produce a programme that responds to the real needs and interests of people in your church.

We like to get letters from others. Write to us if you have something to share related to your experiences in working with people of many ages in your church. We would like to hear about ways this book has been helpful. Also, we would like to hear your own suggestions and ideas.

Don and Pat Griggs   Livermore, California
with Cathy, Scott, and Mark   June, 1976
and Ray and Rhoda Griggs

Introduction

Before I read this book, I would hardly have believed that what it sets out to do could be done in practice. Yet, as I have imagined situations where it could happen, I felt I was on to something very basic to what the Bible is about. So my heart leapt when I read it, and I feel privileged that Bible Society should introduce this book to the British public.

Here in Britain, we labour under three difficulties that make this book a must for us:

1. We find talking about our faith difficult, especially in our families.
2. We are relieved when we think that we can pass on the responsibility for talking about our faith to school and church.
3. Many of us are in relatively small congregations with a rather weak sense of community.

The right combination of difficulties often leads us to a solution. This book could prove to be a vital solution for British churches in the 1980's. It shows us, step-by-step, ways in which we can surmount these three handicaps that we all wish we could overcome. It will help us to get live practice in talking with our children and other families about things that matter to School and Church because we will be "in on the act". We will have a way of making small numbers, with a huge generation gap, productive instead of depressing.

Yet even big congregations need the kind of learning experience provided in this book. Indeed, I think every Christian family at some point in its life needs to work and learn together in this way. If we are a part of this kind of learning we will inevitably grow in confidence and community feeling.

The key to the book is the way in which it uses so many complementary ways of learning to help us understand the Word of God. The power of the story is used both in retelling and sometimes in re-enacting it. Discussion points help to get the text analysed and interpreted. There are ways of helping us to identify with the feelings of biblical characters that show us ways of applying the Bible truths to ourselves. Then the support of the group helps to encourage us to act on what we have learned. These different approaches have been sensitively graded to suit the whole family, so that each is able to contribute or benefit in ways that are natural.

Towards the end of his life, Paul wrote to Timothy: "You know who your teachers were, and you remember that ever since you were a child, you have known the Holy Scriptures", and, " you have the kind of faith that your grandmother Lois and your mother Eunice also had." (2 Timothy 3.14,15; 1.5) We know that Christian teaching in New Testament days was family centred. Using the Griggs book will help us get back to that pattern with great benefits for us all.

Tom Houston
Executive Director
Bible Society

1

Some Basic Concerns

Purpose of the book

We have written this book for:

○ Christian educators who are seeking resources to guide them, and those with whom they work, in thinking about and planning learning activities for mixed age groups.

○ Leaders and teachers of intergenerational programmes who are seeking some specific guidelines, resources, and session plans to help them in their planning and leading.

○ Ministers in small churches where many of the activities in the church's regular programme already involve all ages learning together. We hope that this book will serve as an additional resource in their planning.

○ People in larger churches who are seeking ways to develop some programmes that will bring people from several generations closer together in the life of the church.

○ Denominational leaders who search for resources to recommend to the churches and to the people for whom they are responsible.

The book has three chapters:

1. Some Basic Concerns

In this chapter we attempt to highlight some of the practical administrative and planning concerns that face all who intend to work at developing a programme for generations learning together.

Several of the articles in this chapter are of special importance to those involved in administration:

○ Start with a task group
○ Try a pilot project
○ Some settings for all ages learning together
○ A training event for prospective leaders

Other articles are intended primarily for those who will be leaders or teachers of intergenerational groups:

○ Planning for all ages learning together
○ Cues to increase participation and interaction
○ Getting started with a group

The remaining articles will be of general interest to all who become involved in any way with the whole concept or practice of generations learning together.

2. Learning Activities for All Ages Together

This chapter of session plans is the "heart" of the book. However, if people turn to this chapter without looking at the first chapter they may miss the point. These session plans do not stand alone. They are presented within the framework of some very basic concerns about teaching and learning.

Even though the session plans are organized into nine units it is not intended that a planning committee would use them in the sequence in which they appear. It would be an unusual situation where all the session plans would ever be used.

It is our intention that planners and leaders should select some of these units or sessions to use as the starting point for their planning. The session plans are all samples of what is possible. We would expect people to be selective: to adapt, revise and rearrange what we have written so that it will ''fit'' the local situation.

3. Additional Activities, Resources and Bibliography

In this small chapter people will find a wealth of information. There are some other people and places where resources and information are available to assist with designing teaching strategies for intergenerational groups.

The resources have been checked for availability and we have personal knowledge of each of them. Some of them we have incorporated into our own teaching, and we believe that we can recommend them all without any reservation.

We think that this book could be used in a variety of settings:

○ As a resource book for a denominational or ecumenical training event for key people who are seeking to develop skills and resourcefulness in the whole area of intergenerational learning activities.

○ As a planning guide for a local church committee or task group which is exploring the possibilities of implementing a programme of generations learning together in their own church.

○ As a curriculum resource for leaders and teachers who are leading an intergenerational programme.

1. Some personal experiences

When one attempts to summarize and share personal experiences in print, much is lost in the process. We have been thinking about and working with intergenerational groups in the church for more than ten years. We have experimented with various sizes and structures of groups and tried a wide variety of teaching activities and resources. On the whole we have had good experiences when relating to and leading groups across the ages. We want to share with you some of the things that we have learned, some of our enthusiasm and some of our concerns. But we find it difficult to capture all that it seems important to share in the written word. Perhaps the best we can do is raise a few questions, offer some suggestions, outline some activities, point to some directions, and then trust that you and others in your church will grow together in your own understanding and enthusiasm for generations learning together.

○ Our first experience of teaching children and parents in one class occurred about ten years ago in the Presbyterian Church in Livermore. With the help of a few people and the cooperation of fifteen families we engaged in an experimental programme which we called ''The Junior Experiment''. This programme was described in an article in the March 1969 issue of *Colloquy* magazine. The article is reprinted beginning on page   0. After two years of experimenting with that programme we were convinced that there was great potential for generations learning together. However, Don became involved in other activities so that working directly with families and other intergenerational groups in a local church on a regular basis became more difficult.

○ Whenever we could we tried to find ways to involve people across the ages. In a one week summer conference for those involved in Christian education, we met each day for one and a half hours with children and teachers together. They became one class, working together as fellow learners. Then we spent another ninety minutes just with the teachers. We focused on the concepts, skills, resources and relationships that are basic to Christian education. This proved to be an effective way to train teachers as it gave them the opportunity to experience the learning situation for themselves.

○ For six weeks, before and during Advent, Pat led a programme that was prepared for families and others of all ages. More than one hundred people participated weekly in these forty-five minute sessions. With clear directions, interesting activities for all ages and a lot of helpers, people of all ages became involved together in sharing their feelings and ideas about Advent and Christmas. Many people asked, ''When can we do something like that again?''

○ In a Family Bible Study Retreat that Don led for a neighbouring church we discovered that all the members of a family, and the church family, learn a lot when they do it together, and have a good time doing it. The basic outline of the activities included in that Retreat is presented in Unit 1 beginning on page 45.

○ A similar experience, only on a much larger scale, was when Don and Pat served as part of the leadership team for Family Festival 1972 sponsored by the Reformed Church in America. Here groups of families were to participate in Bible study together. The outline of the three sessions of Bible study for this occasion is presented in Unit 4 beginning on page 81. In both the Retreat and the Festival setting we found that people were able to participate and learn together despite the diversity of ages, interests and backgrounds.

○ Most recently Don has been conducting workshops in various parts of the country on the subject of ''Planning for Intergenerational Learning Experiences''. In each instance people come to the workshop with little experience, but a lot of motivation, in this approach to teaching and learning. As a part of each workshop there is a one-hour period where about a dozen children and young people join us to participate with ten to twelve adults from the workshop in a sample study session. Each time Don leads a group like this, made up of 20-25 strangers, he wonders if it is going to work – and it does. People who participate in the sample session as well as those who watch it are always impressed with how quickly the group becomes a group and how much they enjoy their experiences together. (An outline and description of this workshop is presented on pages 41-44.)

○   Many of the other session outlines come from Pat's teaching in our local church in Livermore with a team of experienced teachers. This class is offered in addition to Sunday School and is called the Celebration Hour. Here children of all ages from about five meet each Sunday with Junior High and Senior High student "helpers" and a variety of adults in a continually changing programme of exploration and study. Units of study are offered in four to eight-week series. This allows for a variety of teaching styles and methods to be used, a continually changing staff, and a number of units of subject matter to be covered. While the programme is offered primarily for the children, it is obvious that the number of older students and adults that are involved in the class make it an intergenerational learning unit. While there may be one or two adults in the class who have done the planning, there may be as many as fifteen other people who have not been involved in the planning but are there learning and growing with the younger students.

2. The Junior Experiment

It is five minutes before ten o'clock on Sunday morning, the opening day of church school in September. I look around the room. Everything is ready. The tables are set for painting. There are plenty of old shirts. The record player is set. I'm nervous, but I guess I am ready.

Five minutes from now, thirty people will be coming from the worship service and all of them, including the parents, will paint. I warned them that this would be an experimental class. But I didn't tell them they'd have to paint the first day!

The first few minutes are a little tense. There are big fathers, dressed-up mothers, and bright-eyed kids. Everyone puts on paint shirts amidst nervous laughter and cautious conversation. The fathers, buttoned into paint shirts, wish there were an escape hatch handy, wondering how they got conned into this. But they are good sports. Everyone responds to my instructions:

"We are going to spend an hour a week together this year learning and growing together. We are going to work hard sharing our ideas, feelings, and questions with one another. There are many ways to communicate. Mostly we use words. But words are often confusing, especially when adults use big words that children cannot understand. So I want you to use the materials on the tables to express your feelings and experiences related to the previous hour of worship. We are not interested in pretty pictures. We are only interested in your own expression through paint of what the worship meant to you. Any questions? Everyone paint."

They start cautiously. Parents feel strange because they haven't done anything like this for years. Children feel a little intimidated because of the adults. One by one, people begin. As each painting is finished, it is displayed

on the wall. Some do a second and third painting. Everyone participates and has fun. One father says, "That was a great experience!" A child comments, "The parents' paintings aren't any better than ours!"

Thus, the Junior Experiment was launched in the First Presbyterian Church of Livermore in the autumn of 1967.

Determining objectives

O Our primary objective in the Junior Experiment was to increase communication between parents and children. Ten and eleven-year-olds are perfect. They have wide interests, are able to express themselves, and understand adults pretty well. But they haven't yet reached adolescence, when they want little to do with their parents.

O A second objective was to include the children as a responsible part of the worshipping, studying, serving community of the church. Too often, church programmes segregate and isolate the generations, contributing more to the gap. Also, the image of the church school is as a child-care centre, while adults do the serious business of being the church. No wonder children don't feel they belong.

O Another objective was to place church education in the context of the family's life in church and home. We live in a time when specialists in every phase of education, recreation, and church life threaten to take the parents' role of nurturing their children. There is evidence that adults and children can be more motivated in church education when they participate together.

O Our fourth objective was to provide opportunities for children and parents to satisfy their natural curiosity and desire to learn by teaching inductively. We were convinced that the only worthwhile learning takes place when people explore ideas, are exposed to various media, and discover those things which give meaning to their own lives.

Designing the programme

There were three major parts to our programme:

Classes for parents and children. This happened on Sunday morning with one hour of worship and forty-five minutes of study. I taught this class, using a variety of resources. There were also several field trips, a swim picnic, and a potluck supper. On these occasions, the other members of the family were also included.

Classes for children. On Wednesdays from 3.45 to 5.15 the children met for study. The period began with games, singing, and refreshments, with an hour and a quarter of study. Two teachers were responsible for this class.

A different parent brought refreshments each week and participated as an observer.

Classes for parents. Once a month I met with parents to discuss the same materials as the children studied on Wednesdays.

Each family paid a £10 tuition fee for the year. This money provided additional resources for each child, child care for teachers' children,

expenses for field trips, a picnic, potluck supper, and curriculum materials.

The most ambitious objectives can look great on paper. But unless they capture the enthusiasm of the participants, you have achieved nothing. That is why planning for the first session was so important. There was a reason for starting with creative painting. Whatever we did during the first session had to motivate adults and children. Anything verbal would probably have reached only one of the groups. There also had to be participation, involvement, and self-expression in order for everyone to feel committed to the class. What better medium than paint? And it proved to be the perfect icebreaker. When all the paintings were posted up, you could not tell which were done by adults and which by children – a great equalizing factor. At the second session, each person shared with the whole class what his painting meant to him. The paintings were not judged but appreciated for what they expressed.

The unit theme for the next ten weeks was worship. Since children worshipped weekly with their parents, they wanted to understand the meaning of what they did. We suspected the parents had something to learn too.

Why do we worship the way we do?

We decided there must be a way for people to recognize the reason for the order of worship. We followed these steps:

1. The teacher asked: "What things do people do that require a certain order or form?"
The class responded: ''Write a letter.'' ''Build a model aeroplane.'' ''Bake a cake.'' ''Cut out and sew a dress.''

The teacher inquired: ''What would happen if we signed our name on the letter before we wrote 'Dear....' or if we did not follow the directions, recipe, or pattern?''

The class responded: ''It wouldn't look right. It would not come out right.''

The teacher agreed and summarized, saying: ''There is a way to bake a cake or build a model. You are right. If we don't follow the directions, we will get confused and it won't come out right. Have any of you ever wondered about the way we do things in our worship service?''

Time was allowed for comments and questions.

2. Then the teacher and his wife did a role-play to illustrate the meaning of the order of worship.
The teacher presented a beautifully wrapped package to his wife. She responded, ''What is this for? It is not my birthday. How come a gift?''

The teacher said, ''I love you and want you to have this gift. Open it.''

''It's a watch. It's beautiful! You shouldn't have done it! What did I do to deserve such a gift? I don't have anything for you. I'm so happy, but I'm sorry I don't have something to give you.''

"Your happiness is enough. I knew you needed a watch, and I wanted you to have one."

Then the man and woman talked for a few minutes, remembering the first watches they had as children, how they felt so grown up, how important watches are, and how valuable time is.

The wife concluded by saying, "I'm so happy, I am going to bake you a cherry pie." She kissed him and the role-play was over.

3. The teacher then gave each person a copy of a bulletin with the order of worship, divided the class into six small groups, and asked them to discuss the question, "What is the connection between the role-play you just saw and the order of worship we follow in church?"

4. After a few minutes of discussion, they said:
○ "God gives us Jesus because he loves us."
○ "We show we are happy with praises and thanksgiving because of God's gift."
○ "Remembering the first watches is like remembering Jesus and the disciples in the scripture and sermon."
○ "What is the point of the cherry pie?"
○ "That is like our gifts to God in comparison to his gift to us."
○ "I see. You really cannot give your offering to God until you have heard and accepted God's gift yourself."

Almost everyone in the class had some reason for why we worship the way we do.

How do you write sermons?

We invited our minister to the class to talk about the many ways he finds ideas for sermons. He also told the class what his topic was for the next Sunday. The class was divided into small groups to think of some questions for him. The minister said he would think about the questions as he prepared his sermon.

The next Sunday, parents and children received a copy of the questions they had asked the previous week. They were asked to write any notes they wanted during the sermon and be prepared to discuss the sermon in class.

Adults and children listened as they never had before. Almost everyone had a page of notes. And they could hardly wait to get to class and discuss them.

Participating in worship

One of the children asked, "Can we help in the service?"

We involved families in many ways. We asked them to serve as greeters for several weeks. We spent one Sunday coaching children to be ushers, and they did an excellent job for a month. One Sunday in class, everyone wrote prayers of confession and thanksgiving and calls to worship. Several prayers were selected and used in the Order of Worship. Here is a prayer of confession, written by a ten-year-old.

"O God, forgive us for living in a nutshell, trying to improve our own lives, while other people are in great need. Forgive us for working too hard to polish ourselves while forgetting what Jesus taught us. Forgive us for wandering from you and your teachings, for travelling alone, for forgetting that you are with us. Hear our prayers in Jesus' name. Amen."

Parent-child conversation

On several occasions, pairs of chairs were placed together in the classroom to allow for conversations between a parent and his child. Prior to Christmas, we followed this procedure:

1. The class was told that for five to ten minutes the parent was to share with the child some of his childhood memories of Christmas. The kids really enjoyed this. Most of them learned something about their parents they had not known.

2. The children were asked to share with the parents what they liked most about Christmas. This gave the parents insight into the children's joys and expectations.

3. Each pair was instructed to choose one favourite family tradition to share with the rest of the class.

4. We spent the last twenty minutes of class sharing these traditions. This sharing provided ideas for other families to consider.

The Bible: the book of the church

After Christmas, the unit of study for the next several months was the Bible. The first Sunday we showed a filmstrip about the Bible. Also, a book about the Bible was given to each family. The whole class was asked to list their questions about the Bible so that we could plan the lessons to answer them. Some of the questions were:

○ "Did God write the Bible?"
○ "Is the creation story true?"
○ "If some of the things in the Bible didn't really happen, why should we believe the Bible?"
○ "How did the Bible begin?"
○ "How long did it take to write the Bible?"
○ "Did the people who wrote the Bible know they were writing scripture?"
○ "Will there ever be any additions to our Bible?"
○ "How could Abraham have lived six hundred years?"
○ "What is the difference between the different versions of the Bible?"

We felt the main idea to get across was that the Bible is the result of the work of many authors. Even on a subject like creation, there are two stories which provide different perspectives. If the class could see this, perhaps they could accept the fact that the Bible is very much the words of men as well as the word of God. To achieve this goal, we planned two basic learning exercises.

Exercise 1

The class was divided into two groups, each with adults and children. Each person was given a photocopied worksheet, divided into three columns, with these questions in the middle column:

1. "How long did creation take?"
2. "Where did creation take place?"
3. "When in the process was man created?"
4. "From what substance were man and woman created?"
5. "What is the relationship between male and female?"
6. "What is the relationship between man and God?"

Heading the first column was Genesis 1.1 — 2.4 and heading the third column was Genesis 2.5-24.

A space was provided for answers. One group was given each of the passages from Genesis. Each group was responsible for answering the same questions based on the content of their passage. They had fifteen minutes to read the passage and answer the questions.

Their answers were not only different but sometimes contradictory. After all the questions were answered, the teacher asked, "Based on the little you know about the beginnings of the Bible and using common sense, how do you account for these differences?" A 10-year-old boy responded, "That's easy! Two different people wrote two different stories and somebody else put them together later."

The point became clear to the whole class. Of the thirty people in the class, only four or five had known there were two accounts of creation and that there was more than one source of the scriptures. Now they all had experienced both stories.

Exercise 2

At the beginning of the next class, the teacher asked for several volunteers to dramatize the point of the previous week's lesson.

A father and his two sons volunteered to be the "model" family. Their only instructions were that they would be brought into the room one at a time and interviewed by the teacher about the younger son's birth.

A woman volunteered to be the recorder. She would record the responses of each family member. Then, after all had responded, she was to present to the class a narrative of the younger child's birth.

The father and older son were dismissed from the room. The younger son was asked questions about the time of day he was born, his father's reactions, his brother's reactions, how his name was chosen. His answers were based on stories he had heard in the family. Then, in turn, the older son and father were asked the same questions. As expected, the answers differed.

Our recorder then gave her account of the younger son's birth. Naturally, she selected some "facts" and left out others. She presented her understanding of the event in a narrative which included some aspects of each person's story. Also, because she felt the mother's perspective was missing, she made up some material to fill in that gap.

The class became excited. They were quick to see the connection between this demonstration and the previous week's discussion.

Again, the inductive, or discovery, approach to learning worked. Parents and children learned. Parents and children were more excited about learning. Parents and children enjoyed learning together.

Many of our objectives were fulfilled. However, we faced some obstacles:
○ There are no resource materials produced for this kind of class. It requires imaginative and innovative teachers.
○ A class of thirty is the maximum size. Many congregations have more than fifteen families. How can we plan to involve more families? Can we justify the time and energy spent on so few?
○ Many teachers, ministers or laymen would not feel comfortable teaching adults and children in the same class.
○ There were many times when the adults talked over the children's heads. The best remedy is for the teacher to say, "Johnny, did you understand what Mr. Jones just said?" "Mr. Jones, would you please repeat what you said so that Johnny can understand you?"

At the end of the year, a child said, "I learned as much about Daddy as I did about the Bible." A mother whose son and husband attended the class said, "I could hardly wait to find out what would happen in Junior Experiment each Sunday. The whole family benefitted from it."

Where do we go from here?

We need versatile, helpful resource materials to use in such classes. We need to try many experiments to discover new teaching approaches in the church. We know the family can learn and grow together; we need to provide more opportunities for it to happen.

3. Start with a task group

Most churches have a committee or person responsible for the Christian education programme in the church. Committees often have more things to discuss than time available for their meetings. In order to start thinking about and planning for intergenerational learning it is important to recruit a special task group to do the work.

Task group membership could include:
○ Representatives from the Church education committee
○ A staff person
○ An experienced Christian teacher or two
○ A couple of parents and grandparents
○ Two or three young people.

The task group may take steps such as the following:

1. Read this book plus several of the resources listed in chapter 3: "Additional Activities, Resources and Bibliography".

2. If possible observe a programme of intergenerational learning in another church in town or nearby.

3. Evaluate the church's present programme in order to identify all the times and places where people of various ages are already involved or where they could become involved.

4. Interview people across the age groups in the church to find out some of the interests and needs that members of the church have that could be focused on in a programme of intergenerational learning.

5. Determine whether or not a programme to involve generations learning together is needed or has the possibility of success in the church.

6. Establish some basic goals for whatever programme may be developed.

7. Design a programme, perhaps a pilot project, for generations to learn together. Decide which age groups will be involved: children and adults, whole families, mixed age groups from various families, or other combinations of ages.

8. Identify the particular skills and traits that are needed by the people who are going to serve as leaders of intergenerational groups.

9. Recruit people to be the leaders. It is best if two people share the leadership of a group of up to twenty-five people. If there are more than twenty-five people then it may be wise to organize two groups each with two leaders.

10. Publicize and promote the programme within the whole congregation. Be sure to interpret the unique goals and features of this programme so that people are clear as to why they are saying "yes" or "no".

11. If possible provide opportunities and/or funds for the leaders to receive additional training to help equip them for their leadership responsibilities.

12. Continue to support and encourage the leaders and participants in the programme. Stay in touch with the programme in order to help with the evaluation after it has been completed.

The steps in this process would be appropriate for a task group on any new programme, not just intergenerational. Our intent is not to suggest that a church's whole programme should become intergenerational, but to suggest some procedures and resources that may contribute to planning for new activities as part of the total church programme.

4. Try a pilot project

Instead of launching a new programme for the whole congregation it may be wiser to start in a small scale with a pilot project. There is a significant advantage to planning for a smaller group, or a shorter time span, in order to test the feasibility of intergenerational activities. It is easier to change, adjust, experiment with, relate to and evaluate a small programme. After working through the whole process with a pilot project it will be easier to anticipate how a larger group will respond and participate. It may be that the original task group would be responsible for the pilot project so that they will know better whether or not to continue their planning to involve a larger portion of the congregation. One possible way to implement the pilot project is outlined below. The pilot project would occur after a task group had accomplished some of the tasks outlined in the previous section.

Step One
Invite people to participate

There are several ways to recruit people to participate in the group. A group of between 20 and 30 people would be best.

○ A couples group or other organization in the church could agree that such a project is something they want to participate in as a major part of their group's programme. They could either volunteer their group to be the planners or leaders, or their families could become the participants.

○ An announcement of the pilot project with an invitation to participate could be published in the church's newsletter or Sunday noticesheet. Be sure to specify the range of ages and whether or not single parent families and singles are included.

○ A representative sample of the members of the church could be selected as potential participants. They could all receive a phone call or letter of invitation to participate. Be sure to include a diversity of ages, family status, and backgrounds.

Step Two
An orientation session

All the people who respond to the invitation to participate will attend an orientation session. The purpose of this session is to explain the reasons for the programme and to outline what people can expect to experience in the programme. All the people who are expected to participate should be invited to the orientation session.

A possible agenda for the orientation session is:
○ A potluck meal
○ A game or other process that helps people get to know each other
○ Singing
○ Someone from the task group outlines the goals and plans for the programme
○ Participants are encouraged to ask questions
○ Leaders of the pilot project are introduced
○ 45-60 minutes experiencing representative sample activities
○ An opportunity for people to indicate whether or not they plan to continue
○ Closing prayer, litany, or song

Step Three
Three to six sessions

Select from this book or another source, or create your own plans, for three to six sessions that will involve between 20 and 30 people of various ages.

The leaders of the three to six sessions should consider seriously the suggestions presented in several other sections of this book. Look at "Planning for all ages learning together," "Cues to increase participation and interaction," and "Getting started with a group."

Step Four
Revise, adjust, and adapt

This is a pilot project. One of the features of a pilot project (the participants should be aware of this also) is that it is experimental, which means that in the midst of the experiment it is possible to revise the plans, adjust the time schedule or adapt to the needs and interest of the participants. It is important for the task group people and the leaders of the programme to stay in communication with each other and with the participants. The participants will be able to offer a lot of feed-back regarding the strengths and weaknesses of the programme based on their own experiences.

Step Five
Evaluation

If the pilot project is intended to precede a larger, more extensive programme, then it is very important to evaluate the programme carefully. Some possibilities to consider in the evaluation process are:

○ Recruit someone at the beginning of the project who will guide the evaluation. This could be a member of the task group.
○ Prepare a questionnaire that all participants, leaders and observers will complete. Keep the questionnaire as simple as possible. Include objective, data-type questions and also some open-ended, subjective questions.
○ Conduct interviews with all, or some, of the participants.
○ Through the questionnaire or interview the evaluator should focus on:
1. General feelings, impressions of the total programme
2. Number of sessions, length of sessions, time of sessions
3. Subject matter
4. Types of activities and resources
5. Value of learning with people of many ages.
○ It is important to receive impressions and reflections on the experience from all ages. Children, youth, adults and older adults will all have different perspectives to bring to the evaluation.

5. Some settings for all ages learning together
Whether you are planning to conduct a pilot project or you intend to have a more extensive programme of intergenerational learning there are a variety of settings that could be considered. The concept and practice of intergenerational learning can be implemented in many different settings. It would be necessary to consider the unique features, needs, and possibilities of each setting and to plan accordingly. Generations can learn together in many different times and places.

Sunday church school

○ In small churches the total church education programme could be intergenerational for all or part of the year.

○ Where church school enrolment is limited to just a few people in each age range in the children's and youth area, it would be possible to involve all ages in one or two classes.

○ In larger churches a special class could be formed for children of one age group with their parents or for a group of families.

○ Another possibility is to combine one adult class with one children's class for a period of three to six weeks.

Family nights

○ Some churches have the custom of monthly family night programmes. Our observation of many of these programmes is that the families share a meal together then the children go one direction for their programme, the youth another direction, and the adults do something else again.

○ It seems to us that the Family Night Programme provides a natural setting to try one or more intergenerational learning activities.

○ After a meal all the families could remain together, or families could be divided into smaller groups, in order to work together in the planned activities.

Holiday Clubs

○ Some churches have had success offering a Holiday Club as an evening programme. It could be one or two weeks, four or five nights each week from 6.30 to 8.30 pm.

○ Or, one night per week through the summer could be planned as Holiday Club night.

○ The whole school could be planned for intergenerational groups or one class could be designated as an intergenerational class.

Retreats or time away together

○ We have found the retreat setting to be a good way to introduce people to intergenerational learning activities.

○ This could be at a conference centre, at a church in another town, or at your own church.

○ This setting provides opportunities for sharing many different activities such as recreation, meals, worship, conversation, and study.

○ These events can last for just one night or for as long as a week.

Short-term contracts

○ A group of families could contract together to meet for a set number of weeks, a specific time for each week, to focus on particular themes or subjects. Part of their contract would include individual and family responsibilities and ground rules for participation in the group.

Days and seasons of the church year

○ Advent, Christmas, Easter, Pentecost and other special days and seasons provide an appropriate occasion for generations to be together for learning, celebrating, and sharing activities.

Using the Bible Series

For All Who Teach

by Donald L. Griggs

○ On a special Sunday, or other day, it would be possible to have an extended period combining study, worship and fellowship where all ages participate in the same programme.

6. Planning for all ages learning together

There are some basic principles and procedures that should be followed when planning for teaching, no matter what the subject or the age group. Don has written a helpful book that people can use when planning Christian education, called *Using the Bible for All Who Teach*. The first eight chapters deal directly with most of the factors that are involved in planning for teaching, and what follows is a summary.

Step one Ask yourself, "What am I going to teach?" To answer that question means that we focus on the key concepts and main ideas that will become the basis for the teaching session.

○ It is better to focus on fewer concepts than to try to "cover" too many. One meaning of "to cover" is "to hide from view, to cover up." That is exactly what happens if we present too many concepts in one session. We cover up a lot of it and thereby hide it from view.

We do not have to cover everything we know on the subject or everything that is in the lesson plan. Our primary responsibility is to uncover what is most important or appropriate for a particular session.

Be selective.

Work at uncovering key concepts.

Don't worry about what has not been uncovered. There will be other sessions, other experiences for more uncovering.

○ It is better to focus on concepts that are more concrete rather than those that are abstract. A concrete concept is something I can identify with personally as a result of my experience. Concrete concepts are based on life experiences. Abstract concepts are more vague, symbols that represent experiences in a more general way. People of all ages are helped more through starting with concrete concepts. Especially in intergenerational groups it is essential that the concepts presented be related to the life experiences of all the people involved.

Keep the concepts simple, concrete, life-centred. Don't become simplistic, just simple.

○ It is better to keep concepts together that belong together. Students of all ages are helped more when concepts and main ideas are clustered around one theme, one event, one person, one experience than when concepts are presented in a random haphazard manner.

○ It is better to develop concepts in a logical, sequential, step by step process than it is to present concepts in a random way.

○ Concepts can be introduced and developed in a variety of ways, through any of the following:

a. a story
b. a question
c. a definition
d. a personal experience
e. a saying or quotation
f. a verse or passage of scripture
g. a picture or other visual aid
h. a report of an event
i. a biography.

○ Teachers need to be open to a wide variety of expressions by participants as they share what they think, believe, feel and value. Remember, concepts are formed by our experiences and everyone has a specific set of unique experiences. We are not seeking unanimity of thought, rather we should value diversity of thought.

Step two Ask yourself, "What will the participants experience and learn?" To answer this question the leader or teacher will need to determine the objectives for the particular session. To set some specific objectives means that the leader intends something to happen to the people who participate: they will be different, think or act differently to some degree by the end of the session. In each of the units and sessions in chapter 2 "Learning Activities For All Ages Together" there is stated a specific set of objectives. (See Editor's Note at the beginning of the book.)

○ Objectives are more specific than goals.

○ Goals are large enough to spend a lifetime pursuing. Goals give us general direction for our teaching and learning. Goals are often beyond our reach. Goals are too general to use for planning and evaluating specific teaching sessions.

Example of a goal:

People will become more loving and caring towards each other.

○ Objectives are more specific, tangible, achievable. Objectives are written in terms of what students can be expected to accomplish in particular learning activities. Objectives are little steps in the direction of a larger goal. Objectives are helpful guidelines for teachers in their planning and evaluating of teaching activities.

Example of an objective:

"At the end of the period of study the participants will visit an elderly person to give them a gift and have a conversation with them."

Step three Answer the question, "What are we going to do to uncover the main ideas and to achieve the objectives?"

Once the key concepts are focused and the instructional objectives determined, the teacher should have a clear sense of direction. The next step in planning is to design the teaching activities that will most effectively communicate the concepts and achieve the objectives. The accent is upon activity.

Often the teacher begins preparation by asking, "What am I going to say to the class about the concept of 'covenant'?" That is the wrong question because answering it leads the teacher to think about what the teacher is going to *tell* the students. A more appropriate question would be "What are the students and I going to *do* about the concept of 'covenant'?"

Answering this question leads directly to thinking about activities and what the participants are going to do to help them learn.

Teaching activities are defined as the actions of students and teachers in the classroom. There are many dozens of possible teaching activities that can be organized into several categories as illustrated by the diagram below.

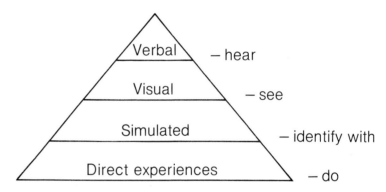

Verbal activities have been the most common means used in teaching. Teaching activities in this category are: lecture, discussion, records, tapes, sermon, story, reading, and any other type of verbal presentation that depends primarily upon the hearing of the learner. The evidence is that most people do not learn well just by hearing something. In order to be effective, verbal activities must be accompanied by other types of experiences. Hearing for most people is a passive activity not requiring much participation from the learner. Also, hearing is very selective. We tend to hear what we want to hear.

Another category of teaching activities is the use of visual symbols. **Visual symbols** involve the learner through seeing. Activities in this category are: use of teaching pictures, filmstrips, map study, films, looking at books, and many other types of visual presentations. Most people learn more from what they see than from what they hear. Seeing is less passive than hearing. Seeing elicits a response from the one who sees. When verbal and visual symbols are used together in a combined activity, the learning is more effective than when either is used separately.

Simulated experiences move us a step further than verbal and visual activities. To simulate is to act out, to act as if a situation that is not real is real. Teaching activities in this category are role play, drama, simulation games, some field trips, some creative writing and other experiences which place students in the position of acting out particular feelings, problems, or issues. One example of a simulated experience using creative writing is where a student assumes the role of Moses at the time he has returned to Egypt to seek freedom for the Hebrew slaves. Moses has confronted Pharaoh, who has refused to let the people go and instead has increased their work load. Pharaoh is uncooperative. The Hebrew people are angry at Moses and Moses wonders whether or not God is going to keep his promise. That is the situation to be simulated. The students are directed to write a letter, as Moses would write, to his wife, father-in-law, or friend back in Midian. A simulated activity involves the students more significantly in developing and identifying with the concepts of the session.

Direct experiences are those activities when students are actually involved in real situations, problems, and concepts. Because so many concepts in religious teaching tend to be abstract it is often difficult to design direct experience teaching activities.

An example in working on the concept of ''love your neighbour as yourself'' would be for the students to visit a Convalescent Home or other shut-ins.

We can talk about ''love your neighbour'' in a long discussion and the chances are that it will make little impression. We could select pictures from magazines to illustrate examples of people caring for others and the meaning would be more memorable. We could act out or write endings to several open-ended stories illustrating people needing love and this gets closer to the meaning of the concept. And we could go as a class, or in small groups, to visit some people who really need love from a neighbour. Which activity would require the most involvement on the part of the student? Which activity would be most memorable? My hunch is that visiting some shut-ins would be remembered by some students for a life-time. Also, the next time the students hear ''and you shall love your neighbour as yourself'' they will probably remember that visit and relate it to the concepts of ''love'' and ''neighbour''.

Step four Decide on the sequence in which the activities will occur.

Every lesson plan has a beginning, middle, and end. There are many alternative activities that are appropriate for beginning, developing and ending a lesson. In what follows several parts of the typical lesson plan are identified specifically.

1. **Opening the session** The first thing that teachers and students do in a session is one of the most important activities of the whole hour. The opening section can be as brief as one minute or as long as ten minutes.

2. **Presenting the subject** Before students can begin to work meaningfully it is helpful to present them with some basic information about the concepts to be developed in the session.

3. **Exploring the subject** Students are more stimulated to learn when they are able to work individually or in small groups to explore further the subject matter that is the focus of the day's session.

4. **Responding creatively** Learning is reinforced and students are able to express themselves when they are encouraged to respond in one or more creative ways to what they have learned.

5. **Concluding the session** Each session should be brought to a fitting conclusion so that students sense a completeness to the sequence of learning activities experienced that day.

All teacher's manuals include the above five categories whether or not they are identified by the same titles. Even though there is something of a logical sequence to these five parts of a lesson plan it is possible that the Presenting, Exploring and Responding activities could be experienced in a variety of combinations. It is possible that Presenting and Exploring activities could happen simultaneously as when students are researching a subject using a variety of sources. Also, Exploring and Responding activities may happen together as when students are writing their own script for selected frames of a filmstrip.

There are many different teaching-learning activities that can be used in each of the above five parts of a lesson plan.

Step five Select resources that will be used to implement whatever teaching activities are planned.

Teaching-learning activities are what teachers and students do in and out of the classroom to experience and communicate particular concepts. Resources are what teachers and students use in the process of teaching and learning.

Resources may be organized in the same categories as described in the preceding section on teaching-learning activities. Examples of resources in each category are:

Resources for verbal activities
○ cassette tapes to listen to
○ cassette recorder for recording students' statements
○ record player for listening to records
○ pens or pencils and paper for writing activities
○ resource books without diagrams, maps or photos (i.e.only with words)

Resources for visual activities
○ maps, charts, posters, photographs and banners
○ filmstrips and projectors
○ overhead projector and transparencies
○ 16mm films and projectors

- ○ 8mm cameras, films and projectors
- ○ blackboard, notice board, whiteboard
- ○ books with photographs, paintings, diagrams, maps
- ○ magazine pictures
- ○ 35mm cameras, slides, projectors
- ○ write-on slides, filmstrips, and films
- ○ flannelgraph, magnetic board.

Resources for simulated activities

- ○ puppets and stage for puppet plays
- ○ directions and supplies for simulation games
- ○ scripts, props, costumes, etc. for dramas
- ○ materials for constructing some scale models
- ○ resources to help students identify with a person, event, or concept.

Resources for direct experience activities

- ○ All the above resources can be used to help students to do something directly related to key concepts that are connected with their own life experiences.
- ○ In addition there are many resources that can help students experience learning directly.

Teachers can gather resources from many places: cupboards at home, or at church, local stores, denominational offices and publishers, and even the dustbin.

Resources can be as costly as a video-tape system and as inexpensive as a magazine.

If students are to be motivated to learn and if they are to use more than verbal symbols to express themselves, then teachers need to use a wide variety of resources.

Resources are as necessary to teaching and learning as dishes and utensils are to eating. You can survive without resources – but not without experiencing considerable frustration.

There are many books, magazines, and articles that suggest creative ways of using a wide variety of resources.

Many teachers have experienced great excitement and satisfaction as they have become involved with other teachers in brainstorming possible ways of using a particular resource.

Criteria for evaluating session plans

After you have created your session plan you could use the following criteria as a basis for evaluating those plans. In the list of criteria you will first read a question that should be asked of your lesson plan, then there is a brief commentary on that question to help you in your evaluation.

1. Is the main idea limited to a few key concepts?
One of the important aspects of planning for teaching is to limit the number

of concepts to be communicated in one session. It is possible for the teacher to "cover" a lot of concepts in one session, but it is much more important for the students to participate in "uncovering" a few key concepts. Keep the concepts connected to each other and related to the students' own experiences.

2. Are the main ideas and objectives appropriate for the age group?
With younger students it is more important to select appropriate parts of a story or event than it is to try to teach the whole story. We need to be sure the students have mastered some of the basic skills before expecting them to achieve more complex objectives. With older students we can deal with abstractions and symbols whereas younger students will be more limited by their concrete thinking.

3. Are the main ideas and objectives directly connected?
It is not surprising to find situations where main ideas and objectives are not directly related to each other. For instance, teachers often select a main idea related to slavery of the Hebrews in Egypt and then select an objective focusing on contemporary forms and situations of slavery. Slavery is the only thing connecting the two, but the historical situations are three thousand years apart. If the main idea of the Hebrews as slaves in Egypt is introduced then the objective should be related to the main idea and not to contemporary forms of slavery. If that objective is intended then a related main idea should be selected. It would be possible to use both main ideas and both objectives even in the same session.

4. Which types of teaching activities and resources are to be used?
In reviewing all the teaching activities and resources that are planned there should be a balance of verbal, visual, simulated and direct experiences. If there is a heavy use of just verbal activities and resources then the plan is out of balance. There needs to be a blending of all the different types of experiences.

5. What kinds of questions did the teachers ask during the session?
There are at least three categories of questions which include information, analytical and personal questions. All three types of questions should be asked during the session. If there are more information questions than the other two categories, then the students are not being encouraged to think enough and apply the subject matter to their own lives.

6. What choices did the students have the chance to make during the session?
Every student should have the opportunity to make a number of choices during the sessions. Students are more motivated and more involved when

they are encouraged to make choices during the session. Some choices are little, like deciding which book to read or which colours to use to express a feeling. Other choices may be big, like deciding how to interpret a passage of scripture or deciding how to act in a particular situation. Little or big, students need many opportunities to make choices.

7. Are there a variety of activities and resources planned for the session?

A one activity lesson is a dull lesson. Students have different abilities, interests, and needs so that teachers must plan for a variety of activities and resources in order to respond to these differences. Students need a change of pace, they need to build from one activity to the next in order to remain interested.

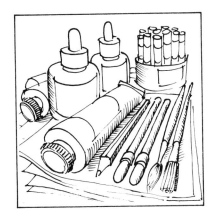

8. If the students are expected to do something new, have they had a chance to practise or experiment?

Teachers should regularly introduce new activities and resources for the students to use in their exploring and creating. In order to ensure the student's success with new activities and resources, there needs to be a time for practice and experimentation where students can find out for themselves how to do or use what the teacher has planned. The same principle applies to the teacher who plans to use a new resource or try a new activity. There needs to be time allowed for previewing, practising and experimenting by the teacher.

9. Has the room been arranged so that it helps the objective to be achieved?

Arrangement of tables and chairs; placing of learning centres, activity corners and resource equipment; display of visual materials on the wall, notice board or blackboard; and easy accessibility of all necessary supplies: all contribute significantly to the smooth functioning of the class and achievement of the intended objectives. Look at your room before the students arrive. What does the room say to you? It should speak very loudly of what is expected to happen in that session. The room arrangement needs to be changed regularly, sometimes as often as weekly.

10. How much time will be required for each of the planned activities?

The best lesson plan ever can be "shot-down" if sufficient time has not been allowed for each activity. Be realistic about time. Allow enough time for students to work without being rushed. Be flexible enough to adjust the schedule if necessary. Also, plan for some additional activities for those students who work more quickly or have more ability.

By applying these questions to the plans you have made it should be possible to evaluate what you have planned before trying to teach it. If you can discuss the plan with someone else you should be able to get enough feedback for your responses to questions to be realistic. Consider reworking some of your plans before you enter the classroom to teach them.

7. Cues to increase participation and interaction

A programme for generations learning together will not work unless the leaders are able to develop and practise some very basic, effective communication skills. People who can teach adults, or other people who are effective as teachers of children or young people, are not necessarily competent and comfortable in a teaching-learning setting that involves people from several age groups at different stages of growth. However, a teacher who is an effective communicator with one age group may, with some training and practice, develop the skills necessary to work with intergenerational groups.

There are some very basic principles of communication which can be implemented in any class, no matter what the age group. It is especially important that these principles be practised where several age groups are together. The principles will be represented as a series of cues which are outlined below. The reason for practising these cues is in order to increase the participation and interaction of all the members of the group.

Cue 1 – Leaders are not necessarily experts

To volunteer to be a leader for an intergenerational group that will spend time together in a variety of learning activities does not require that one be an expert in specific subject matter or even in group processes. The leader needs to be one who has time to spend planning, who enjoys people of all ages, who is sensitive to the needs and interests of others and who is open to the ideas and expressions of others.

Cue 2 – People have names

Leaders need to call on people and refer to them by name. This not only reinforces the person but also sets a model for others to follow. Children and others who have a hard time remembering names will be helped when they hear people's names repeated. Name tags may be helpful at the beginning, but it is important to really learn people's names and not continually depend upon the name tag.

The leaders and/or group will have to decide early on how children will address the adults. Some groups feel strongly that everyone should be addressed by their first name by all ages. Others feel just as strongly that children should address adults as Mr, Mrs, and Miss.

Cue 3 – Families don't always have to stay together

For some activities, and for some families, it will be important for the family to stay together. It may be important during the first couple of sessions that

families be together. However, one of the values of generations learning together is the opportunity for people of all ages to encounter others from different age groups, different family customs, with different personal interests. Children, especially, need to interact with adults other than their parents. And single people, older adults and others without families in the community need the enrichment of relationships with others of all ages.

Plan activities that provide occasional opportunities for people to regroup themselves other than in family groups.

Cue 4 – Balance individual, small and large group activities

A session that is totally devoted to large group activities or emphasizes only small group activities is a session that is out of balance. One session may feature one type of activity more than another, but there should always be some individual, some small group and some large group activities during a session, or series of sessions.

Activity	Advantages	Disadvantages
Individual activities	People can work at their own pace. People can choose what is of personal interest. Leader may be able to seek opportunity to relate to individuals.	No opportunity for interaction with others. People are not challenged by the ideas and feelings of others.
Small group activity	People are more involved with each other. Exposure to different ideas, feelings, values. Develop skills of cooperation, negotiation and planning.	Assertive, verbal people may dominate. If adults become leaders children may withdraw, depending on the sensitivity of the leader. May take a lot of time.
Large group activity	Takes less total time. Everyone experiences the same thing. The best way to present films, filmstrips, and other "input" activities. Worship, games, meals, simulation activities and other similar experiences work well when the whole group is together.	The quieter, less verbal people get lost in the group. Hard for leader to be aware of how all the people are responding. People may not be able to make their own choices about what and how to do things. Individuals may lose interest.

Cue 5 – Choices increase motivation

People who are able to make choices about what and how they are going to learn, and with whom they are to do it, are more motivated than those who are *told* what to do. When we have people with so many different abilities, interests, and needs as we have in an intergenerational setting it is especially important that we plan for people to make as many choices as possible.

People can make choices when they:
O decide where to sit
O select which person to work with
O choose which materials to use in order to do a creative activity
O answer questions in their own words
O decide which resource books to use in their study
O elect which learning centre or activity to work at
O choose a role with which to identify
O rank items in their own personal order of priority
O decide which scripture passages to read or which Bible to use.

Cue 6 – Provide a common starting place

Leaders will be helpful to both younger and older learners if a common starting place is provided for all to experience together. It is better not to assume that the participants already have prior knowledge or experience. Even if a subject is presented that is familiar to a few people it may be that they will still get some new insights or find that what they knew previously is being reinforced.

A common starting place may be:
O a passage of scripture read by the leader or individually
O a film or filmstrip
O a verbal presentation
O a series of questions or activities on a worksheet
O a story which is told or read or acted out
O something on a cassette recording for all to hear
O a photograph, painting, teaching picture or other visual
O a definition from a book or printed on a chart
O tasks outlined in a worksheet
O words from a song, poem, or speech.

Cue 7 – Be sure instructions are clear

With people representing a wide range of abilities, interests and experiences, some will need very clear, step-by-step instructions for most activities. Others may need only a general suggestion of how to do an activity or what is expected. For the sake of the whole group it is important to provide simple, step-by-step clearly stated instructions. Instructions are best when they are written so that everyone can read them and then work at their own pace. Write instructions on newsprint, poster board, blackboard, photocopied sheet, or overhead transparency.

Cue 8 – Make it visible
People understand much more when they can see as well as hear. Charts, diagrams, pictures, photographs, overhead projection, and other visual presentations are very helpful. When listening to an unfamiliar song it is helpful to have the words printed so all can read while listening. When presenting a biblical story it will help both adults and children to focus on the story if you use a film, filmstrip, or teaching picture that presents the story visually.

Cue 9 – Everyone can be creative
To be creative does not mean that one has to be an artist. It does mean that one has some ideas and feelings that are personal and special that can be expressed in any of several dozen creative ways. The leaders do not need to be creative with music, painting, writing, or drama in order to facilitate others expressing themselves in those creative media. The leaders only need to provide the setting, the materials, and the motivation so that others can choose which medium to use in order to create their own verbal, visual, or enacted expressions.

Creative activities are not busy-work. Creative activities are the means by which people express their own personal affirmations of what they think, feel, believe and value.

Cue 10 – Share what has been created
There is value for a person just in the process of creating, but there is increased value for that person and others in the group when what was created is shared. The sharing may be with the whole group as part of a closing presentation, or it may be with one another or a few people in an informal way. Creative expressions can be shared by mounting on a display board, photocopying or displaying on a table.

Cue 11 – Don't be afraid of feelings
Much Christian education tends to focus on facts, doctrines, events, and interpretations. This can all be interesting but it may never reach the level of people's emotions and affections. Feelings are universal. We can connect with biblical people more directly at the feeling level than at any other. We can come closer to other people in our group when we share our feelings with each other. There may be times when strong feelings get expressed in

a group that cause us to be somewhat uncomfortable. However, better to risk being uncomfortable than to suppress or neglect the importance of sharing at the feeling level.

Cue 12 – Accept ideas and feelings

When teachers, leaders and others are able to accept the ideas or feelings expressed by people in the group there is much more opportunity for interaction. We can accept ideas and feelings expressed by others without necessarily having to agree with them. When people sense that they are accepted they are much more willing and able to participate. We can show our acceptance in several ways:

○ non-verbally, with a smile, nod or other gesture
○ by reflecting back what someone has said
○ by asking people to clarify what they meant by what they said
○ by identifying with them through reflecting on our own personal experiences that are similar.

Cue 13 – Ask open questions

Closed questions have right and wrong answers. Answering closed questions feels like taking a test. It is impossible to have a discussion with closed questions. Information is important but it can be presented in many ways without having to ask a series of closed, informational questions.

Open questions lead to discussion. Open questions require more in the way of analytical thinking and personalized application. There are usually a variety of possible ''right answers'' to an open question. Open questions are prefaced by phrases such as:

○ ''Why do you suppose...?''
○ ''What are some possibilities of...?''
○ ''How does that compare with...?''
○ ''Why do you think...?''
○ ''What are some examples of...?''
○ ''What is an occasion when...?''
○ ''When you think of _____ what comes to mind...?''
○ ''What would you think if...?''
○ ''How would you act in the situation if...?''

Cue 14 – Ask for clarification

If a person answers a question or makes a statement with a very brief response you will almost always be safe in assuming that the person has more to offer than the brief statement. The teacher or leader can respond to the brief statement with a request that the student say a little more, clarify, expand on his original statement. More times than not the person will have more to say.

Also, there are times when a student answers a question or makes a statement and we do not understand what was meant. Here again we can ask for clarification, "Say a little more about what you meant by..." or, "I don't quite understand, help me to see what you mean by..."

Leaders need to be sensitive to adult answers and statements and ask for clarification, sometimes not because the *leader* does not understand, but because there is the possibility that the *children* may not understand. This is especially true in the beginning when children may be hesitant to admit they don't understand or to ask quesions. Adults need to be reminded to express themselves so that everyone understands them.

Cue 15 – Listening is important

Teachers and leaders need to listen as much as, or perhaps even more than, the participants in their groups. Instead of being anxious about what we want to tell or ask the other person, it will be better just to listen to what the other person is saying and then after listening figure out a way to respond. People will know we are listening when we look directly at them and are not distracted with other interests, and when we respond in non-verbal or verbal ways that show we are hearing them. In intergenerational groups, leaders will have to work hard at helping children to listen to adults and especially to get the adults really to listen to the children.

Cue 16 – Silence is all right

If the leader asks a good, open question and there is not an immediate response, the worst thing the leader can do is to break the silence with an answer, or with more questions. If it is a good question it will take time to think through an answer. Ten to fifteen seconds is not a very long time for thinking. Yet the average teacher cannot tolerate more than five seconds of silence after a question. Silence is all right. Let the participants "feel the burden" of the silence. They will respond when they realize they are responsible for the silence instead of waiting for the leader to break the silence.

Cue 17 – Everyone has a right to "pass"

There is no special virtue in having all participants speak up or express themselves whenever there is an opportunity. It is especially disturbing to go around the circle expecting every person to share something in turn. The poor person who is tenth in line had six good ideas but they were all shared before his turn. That person feels as if he/she has failed. Instead the teacher is the one who failed by setting up the activity in that way. People should have the right to "pass", to not share anything if they choose not to. In their choosing not to share they should not be made to feel as if they have failed. It is better to ask a question or offer a task to the whole group than to go around the circle or call on one specific person.

8. Getting started with a group

Even though we live in families, which are by nature intergenerational, most of us do not have many experiences where children, young people and adults are all involved in a programme where each is a participant with equal standing and responsibility. Since this may be a new experience for most people it is very important that the groups get started in such a way that everyone feels a part of the group. "Getting started" activities will help establish the tone of the whole programme. Several things can be achieved by effective "getting started" activities:

○ People will become involved quickly in a non-threatening, fun way.
○ People will begin to get to know each other.
○ A style of leadership and participation will be established.
○ People of various ages will have opportunity to mix with each other.

The leader needs to be as relaxed and flexible as possible when getting started with a group. This is asking a lot, because most leaders will be very anxious about the first couple of sessions with a new group and a new type of programme. However, if the planning has been carefully and thoroughly done the leader can be free to respond to the people in the group and their needs, showing confidence in the process and the plans that have been made. This confidence will facilitate an atmosphere of trust and will lead the whole group to be relaxed about the class. After a few weeks when this level is reached, the leader and participants may want to talk about their feelings toward the whole programme.

When selecting a "getting started" activity the leader should pick one that he or she feels happy with. The process of the activity should be clear, the directions should be well thought out, and some problems may be anticipated along with responses to the problems. Select an activity that you feel confident will work with your particular group.

Some possible "getting started" activities are:

A. Match facts to people

1. Give each person three or four 3″ x 5″ cards or similar size pieces of paper. Each person also needs a pencil.
2. Instruct each person to write one fact about himself or herself on each card. Some suggested categories are: a hobby, a place visited, a funny experience, something about a trip or vacation, a favourite pet or sport, or something else. Write a different fact on each card. Younger children may need help from parents.
3. After all the cards are completed everyone places all their cards in the centre of the room. Turn cards upside down and scramb
4. Then, each person draws out of the pile as many cards a you draw your own card, put it back and draw another.
5. Now, circulate among the group trying to find the cards belong. This usually takes some time. And th informal visiting happens. Younger children

encouragement to get started. Encourage them to feel free to approach adults as well as other children.

6. When a person finds a match to the card write that person's name on the card so that the information can be used to introduce the person later.

7. After everyone has identified the ''owners'' of their cards sit in a circle and begin to introduce people one by one.

8. The leader will have a list of all the members of the group. Read one name at a time. People who have cards with information about the person whose name was read out will read the information on the cards and share any other bits of information about that person.

The value of this process is that everyone is involved in a personal way, encountering everyone in the group in brief, one-to-one encounters. People decide for themselves what they want to share with the whole group about themselves. And, with such a variety of personal anecdotes being presented, people in the group will identify others with whom they may want to have further conversation.

Don't rush this getting acquainted process. It is important!

B. Circle within a circle

1. Organize the whole group into two circles, one circle standing inside the other circle. Both circles should have equal numbers of people.

2. The inside circle turns round to face the outside circle, which means that each person should be standing face to face with someone else. If there is an uneven number in the group, the leader can participate to make the circles even.

3. The leader says something like, ''The outside circle move three people to the left and talk for one minute about where you were born.''

4. This process is repeated for as many times as the leader chooses. Move ''x'' number of people to left or right so that each time people end up face to face with someone different.

5. Some possible topics for quick conversation are:
○ What is your favourite TV show?
○ One thing you did this last summer.
○ What musical instrument do you play or like the best?
○ One vegetable you don't like and one you do like.
○ Someone who is a hero to you.
○ A place in the world you would like to visit.
○ A famous person you would like to meet.
○ A favourite place to eat away from home.
○ If you had £100 what would you buy?
(Keep the conversations limited to one minute each.)

1. The leader introduces the activity by giving an example: ''When I mention two things, like sailing or surfing, which would you like to do most,

go sailing on a lake or go surfing in the ocean?''

2. Each person chooses one or other of the alternatives.

3. Leader identifies one side of the room for one choice and the other side for the other choice.

4. People go to the side of the room which represents their choice.

5. Each person meets with another person who made the same choice.

6. For one minute each they share with each other why they chose that particular item.

7. Then the leader calls ''time'' and gives another pair of items from which people must choose one. Some example of other choices are:

○ Eating at McDonalds or an Italian restaurant
○ Hiking in the mountains or cycling along the open road
○ Working in an ice-cream shop or a toy store
○ Spending time at a library or a museum
○ Taking a trip on a plane or a boat
○ Visiting friends in the city or on a farm

D. People scavenger hunt

1. Leader prepares a duplicated sheet listing the kinds of things we might be able to find out about other people.

2. Each participant receives a list for the scavenger hunt and then tries to find someone who matches the descriptions.

3. When someone is found who matches a description their name is written in the blank space.

4. People try to fill in all of the blanks in the time that is given.

5. When the leader calls ''time'' the group gathers. The leader reads off each item. Everyone who has a name in that blank reads the name and then the person whose name is called stands up. If anyone else thinks that item ''fits'' them, they can call out their name and stand up also.

6. A sample list of items (make up your own to be appropriate for your group).

Find:

a. Someone with hazel eyes _____

b. An eldest child in a family _____

c. The tallest person in the group _____

d. The person with the longest surname _____

e. A person born outside the United Kingdom _____

f. A person whose first name begins with ''C'' _____

g. One of the leaders of the group _____

h. A person who is a football fan _____

i. A person born in this town _____

j. A person who likes to read _____

k. A person wearing glasses _____

l. Someone who plays the piano _____

m. Someone who likes to watch sports on TV _____

n. An adult who walked a mile to school as a child _____
o. The youngest person who is an aunt or uncle _____
p. A person who likes to play tennis _____
q. The person with the shortest first name _____
r. Someone who likes to eat pizza _____
s. Someone who owns a stereo radio _____
t. The child who walks the farthest to school _____
u. _____
v. _____
w. _____
x. _____
y. _____
z. _____

(add some of your own)

9. A training event for prospective leaders

It is possible that a church, a group of churches or a denominational group will want to plan a training event for prospective leaders. The outline which follows is from a six-hour workshop which Don has conducted several times. This outline is presented to serve only as a sample of what is possible. It is important for each planning group to design their own workshop to respond to the interests and needs of the people in their group.

Generations learning together
(A sample six-hour workshop)

The opening
1. Greetings and introductions
2. A get-acquainted activity – in groups of three to five, share with each other something you have enjoyed doing where more than one generation was involved.
3. Each small group write down the experiences mentioned. Write a phrase about each on a piece of newsprint. Mount the newsprint on the wall.
4. Spend a few minutes where everyone will browse among the lists of experiences that are mounted.

Introductory presentation
The leader will offer some brief comments that may include references to:
○ A developing, widespread interest in family groups and other intergenerational activities in churches.
○ Decline, disruption and disintegration of the family in Britain – especially the extended family, also the nuclear family.
○ Church tends to be a place and programme that separates family members, and age groups, from each other.
○ Church can be a place and programme that brings families, and age groups, together in learning, worship, fellowship and service activities.
○ Some personal experiences and impressions.

Brainstorm life-centred experiences

Activities planned for intergenerational groups must focus on life-centred experiences if we are going to involve people of all ages.

1. In two minutes, each person writes down words or phrases that represent personal, family, community, or church experiences that are common to people of all ages. (These are what we mean by life-centred experiences.) They can be used as a basis for planning "curriculum" for intergenerational groups.

2. Each person selects the two or three most important experiences on his or her list.

3. In small groups of three to five people compare and share each person's top two or three experiences.

4. Develop a composite list by asking each person to mention the experience that they have shared. The workshop leader should write them all down on newsprint or an overhead projector to form a composite list that the group can focus on.

5. The leader can make a few comments to summarize what is included on the list. Or perhaps someone in the group will have some comments to make.

Samples of life-centred experiences mentioned by one group:

family	memories	children
birth	birthday	mistakes
home	church	school
gifts	parents	vacation
pets	meals	leading
games	work	reunions
winning	losing	anniversaries
friends	enemies	parties
death	following	wind/rain/snow
travelling		

Planning for generations learning together

Work in small groups of two or three people.

The leader introduces one step at a time. Explain what is expected at each step. Be sure that instructions for each step are visible on a chart or transparency so that people will have something to refer to while they are working.

Step 1 Select one life-centred experience from the composite list to be the focus for your planning.

Step 2 Explore in Bibles and other resource books for some biblical-theological reference points.

Step 3 Write a paragraph that states what you think is central to the experience and how it connects with the Christian life.

Step 4 Write out several objectives for participants to accomplish as a result of spending time focusing on the subject.

Step 5 Brainstorm some possible activities and resources to help you to communicate the experience you have centred on.

Step 6 Plan a strategy that includes opening, exploring, creating and closing activities.

Step 7 Prepare a sheet with all the necessary instructions etc. so that each member of the group can have one.

It usually takes about an hour and a half to accomplish all seven steps.

A sample session of generations learning together

About ten to twelve children and young people of various ages need to be recruited before the event. Also, ten to twelve people from the workshop group need to be recruited to participate with the children and young people in a sample session of learning activities.

The others in the workshop group can be observers. They should scatter themselves throughout the room. As observers they should remain silent during the entire session. They can take notes to guide their comments and question-asking after the sample session.

It is possible that this part of the workshop could happen earlier in the day. It all depends upon the time of day the children and young people are available.

The content for the sample session can be taken from one of the session outlines in this book or from another source. It should be simple enough to do in an hour, and representative enough to include a variety of aspects of the whole process of generations learning together. Also, the sample session has to be complete in itself.

Be sure to include a brief getting-acquainted time at the beginning of the session because you will be working with a lot of strangers.

Reflection and discussion

The following questions could guide a discussion to follow the sample session.

○ What did you see happen?

○ What are some problems with this style? What are the implications of those problems?

○ What are some values of this style and structure of teaching and learning?

○ What is the role of the teacher or leader?

○ What is the relationship between what was demonstrated and the earlier experience of planning focused on a life-centred experience?

○ If you were to begin planning for this type of teaching-learning in your church:

a. What questions would you ask?

b. What are the first steps you would take?

○ What strategy could be used to help people in the church to develop a programme of generations learning together?

2 Learning Activities for All Ages Together

Each set of activities for all ages together will need careful planning, so it is best to get together a local planning team who will be familiar with the schedules, space, resources and budget of their church or churches.It is our hope that the previous chapters will have provided some guidelines for those responsible for planning.

What follows is a series of outlines of learning activities that could be used or adapted by a planning team as they prepare for intergenerational learning in their church. These outlines are intended to be "starters" in the planning process. The activities have been used by Don and Pat Griggs in a variety of settings. However, to be used by other people in different settings it is very important that these activities be revised, adapted and tailored to fit the unique circumstances of the local situation.

Each outline of a unit of study includes several items:

A. Introduction

In this section we will set the stage by focusing on the theme or main idea of the session with some words of orientation and description.

B. Objectives

Each session or unit of sessions will include several objectives. The objectives are basic to planning and evaluation. Not all participants will achieve all the objectives. Some objectives will be more appropriate for younger learners and other objectives are directed to older learners.

C. Materials needed

All activities require some resources to be used by and with participants.

D. Sequence of activities

Each session and unit will be outlined with a sequence of activities that develops the theme and seeks to involve all the participants in a variety of ways.

Unit 1: Developing Bible Skills

A. Introduction

This unit was used with a group of thirty people. The youngest was six years old. There were about eight under tens, five young people and the rest were adults. There were nine families represented by one or more of their members. The unit was designed for people with reading skills, so when a six-year-old child turned up we were surprised. The parents felt that their son would be all right and would have a good time even though he could not read well. That proved to be true, since there were a lot of filmstrips and books with stories and pictures. Also, the six-year-old was free to participate or not according to how he and his parents decided.

Since this unit depends upon reading skills, older learners were encouraged to team up with younger learners to provide the skills that were necessary to complete the planned activities. Reading aloud, exchanging ideas, asking and answering questions, and searching together for information became the norm for the class. The learners of all ages became "teachers" for each other.

We believe that it is important for students of all ages in the church to develop skills that will help them in studying the Bible. Children receive Bibles as prizes in many churches. Parents and young people have often either not learned basic Bible skills or have not practised them in order to maintain the skills. With this being true of people in many churches, we think a unit focusing on Bible skills can be very helpful and also a lot of fun. Our experience has been that all learners with the ability to read and to do some limited research are motivated to participate and get a lot of satisfaction from activities as outlined below.

B. Unit objectives
At the end of this unit participants should be able to:
O Describe six to ten specific features of the Bible that make it different from other books.
O Show another person how to use a Bible Concordance.
O Find a passage of scripture by using cross-reference footnotes.
O Find a key word in a Bible Dictionary and write or state a definition of that word in their own words.
O Use Bible resource books to find information about people and places in the Bible.

C. Materials needed
O Bibles with study helps
O Concise Concordances
O Bible resource books – Dictionaries, Atlases, story books, etc. (see Bibliography)
O Pencils, paper, felt pens, construction paper

D. Sequence of activities
This unit was prepared for a weekend family retreat. We had a total of five to six hours for the activities outlined here. To use this unit in a weekly setting of one-hour sessions the activities must be carefully tailored to fit the time, space, class, etc.

Activity One: Getting acquainted
When we did this unit it was the first time that the group had been together. We spent the first fifteen minutes getting to know each other. We made name tags with "-ing words" on them and then used the "Circle in a Circle" activity. (See page 37 where some suggestions are offered for getting started with a group.)

Activity Two: Observations of the Bible
1. Work in family groups or other mixed age groups of three to five people.
2. Each person needs a Bible.
3. The leader can give the following instructions:
○ Look at the Bible, and flip through the pages.
○ Make a list of the many things you notice about the Bible.
○ Take five minutes to work as a group to make a list of as many observations as you can of what you notice about the Bible. There are no wrong answers. (Someone in each group should record on a piece of paper all the group's observations.)
4. After five minutes the leader calls "Time" then begins to make a composite list of Bible observations. Write the list on an overhead transparency, sheet of newsprint or blackboard. Encourage groups to take

turns in offering their observations so that each group will have equal opportunity to make their contributions.

5. The leader can then summarize by commenting on:

○ How much the group know about the Bible.

○ How unique and different the Bible is from other books.

○ How observant they were.

Activity Three: Questions about the Bible

1. Participants continue in the same small groups.

2. Each person writes on a slip of paper one or two questions about the Bible. Non-readers and those who are learning to read will have some questions even if they cannot write them down. Someone in each group should serve as a "scribe" for these people.

3. Groups exchange questions with each other. Each group reads their new set of questions and selects several questions to share with the whole class.

4. Make a composite list of questions from all the groups. Record questions on overhead transparency, blackboard or newsprint so that everyone can see all questions.

5. Leader can respond to the composite list of questions. There may be a few questions that could be answered directly by the leader. However, his comments may be more appropriate if they include the following:

○ All these questions are good questions.

○ Although we might wish someone would give us all the answers, it is important that we work at finding our own answers.

○ We need to learn how to use Bible study tools and to discover which tools will help us with particular questions.

○ After practising with the tools and doing some research we will return to our list of questions to share some of our discoveries.

Activity Four: Bible Concordances

Sometimes we have questions about where to find particular Bible passages or we want additional passages on a specific subject. A Bible Concordance is a very helpful tool in finding Bible passages.

1. Each participant, or pair of participants, should have a Bible Concordance in front of him.

2. Show on a chart or transparency the following definition:

"A Concordance is an alphabetical list of the important words in a book with references to the passages in which they occur."

3. Before using a Concordance, instruct participants to find the Lord's Prayer in the Bible. (Some people will need help to do this.)

Whether people have difficulty finding the Lord's Prayer or not, the leader can comment:

○ Some passages we may be able to find, but we are limited if we depend on our memory to find passages in the Bible.

○ We are also limited if we depend on flipping through the pages to find a passage.

○ To find something specific we need the help of a person who knows where it is, or we need a "tool" like a Concordance.

4. Now use the Concordance. Turn to the word **prayer.** Notice there are lots of verses listed under that word. But we will not find the words "Lord's Prayer" in most Concordances because that is a *title* given to a prayer.

We need to look under words that are a part of the prayer itself. What are some words that might help us, especially if the well-known words are not exactly the same in a modern translation?

The participants may suggest words such as: Father, heaven, kingdom, earth, forgive, etc.

Here is an example of the references listed under "Heaven" in the Concordance to the *Good News Bible.*

Mt 3.16	Then **heaven** was opened to him, and he saw the Spirit of
3.17	Then a voice said from **heaven,** "This is my own dear Son,
5.12	and glad, for a great reward is kept for you in **heaven.**
5.16	the good things you do and praise your Father in **heaven.**
5.34	Do not swear by **heaven,** for it is God's throne;
5.45	so that you may become the sons of your Father in **heaven.**
5.48	You must be perfect – just as your Father in **heaven** is perfect!
6. 1	you will not have any reward from your Father in **heaven.**
→6. 9	"Our Father in **heaven:**
6.10	may your will be done on earth as it is in **heaven.**
6.14	done to you, your Father in **heaven** will also forgive you.
6.20	up riches for yourselves in **heaven,** where moths and rust cannot
6.26	yet your Father in **heaven** takes care of them!
6.32	Your Father in **heaven** knows that you need all these things.
7.11	then, will your Father in **heaven** give good things to those
7.21	those who do what my Father in **heaven** wants them to do.
10.32	I will do the same for him before my Father in **heaven.**
10.33	me publicly, I will reject him before my Father in **heaven.**
11.23	Did you want to lift yourself up to **heaven?**

5. You may sometimes need to look up more than one word before you find the passage you are looking for. It depends on how full the Concordance is.

6. In order to provide an opportunity to practise the skill of using the Concordance, encourage participants to suggest some verses they recall but do not know where to find in the Bible. After searching for half a dozen verses the skill should be reinforced enough for everyone to feel confident in using a Concordance.

A word of caution: If you are using a Concise Concordance you will not always find every verse you look for. A Concise Concordance is limited in that it only includes the more familiar passages.

Activity Five: Bible cross-references

1. Jesus was asked by someone: "Which is the great commandment in the law?" Jesus answered, "Love the Lord your God with all your heart, with all your soul, and with all your mind."

2. Using a Concordance, find this passage in the Gospel of Matthew in the *Good News Bible.*

3. Leader introduces the parallel references under the section headings, and the cross-reference footnotes at the bottom of the page. Notice that the bold print numbers at the bottom are the verses in Matthew, and the light print text following is where this verse is featured in other places in the Bible. Here is an extract from the *Good News Bible.*

I invited did not deserve it. ⁹Now go to the main streets and invite to the feast as many people as you find.' ¹⁰So the servants went out into the streets and gathered all the people they could find, good and bad alike; and the wedding hall was filled with people.

11 "The king went in to look at the guests and saw a man who was not wearing wedding clothes. ¹²'Friend, how did you get in here without wedding clothes?' the king asked him. But the man said nothing. ¹³Then the king told the servants, 'Tie him up hand and foot, and throw him outside in the dark. There he will cry and grind his teeth.' "

14 And Jesus concluded, "Many are invited, but few are chosen."

The Question about Paying Taxes
(Mark 12.13–17; Luke 20.20–26)

15 The Pharisees went off and made a plan to trap Jesus with questions. ¹⁶Then they sent to him some of their disciples and some members of Herod's party. "Teacher," they said, "we know that you tell the truth. You teach the truth about God's will for man, without worrying about what people think, because you pay no attention to a man's status. ¹⁷Tell us, then, what do you think? Is it against our Law to pay taxes to the Roman Emperor, or not?"

18 Jesus, however, was aware of their evil plan, and so he said, "You hypocrites! Why are you trying to trap me? ¹⁹Show me the coin for paying the tax!"

They brought him the coin, ²⁰and he asked them, "Whose face and name are these?"

21 "The Emperor's," they answered.

So Jesus said to them, "Well, then, pay the Emperor what belongs to the Emperor, and pay God what belongs to God."

22 When they heard this, they were amazed; and they left him and went away.

The Question about Rising from Death
(Mark 12.18–27; Luke 20.27–40)

23 That same day some Sadducees came to Jesus and claimed that people will not rise from death. ²⁴"Teacher," they said, "Moses said that if a man who has no children dies, his brother must marry the widow so that they can have children who will be considered the dead man's children. ²⁵Now, there were seven brothers who used to live here. The eldest

got married and died without having children, so he left his widow to his brother. ²⁶The same thing happened to the second brother, to the third, and finally to all seven. ²⁷Last of all, the woman died. ²⁸Now, on the day when the dead rise to life, whose wife will she be? All of them had married her."

29 Jesus answered them, "How wrong you are! It is because you don't know the Scriptures or God's power. ³⁰For when the dead rise to life, they will be like the angels in heaven and will not marry. ³¹Now, as for the dead rising to life: haven't you ever read what God has told you? He said, ³²'I am the God of Abraham, the God of Isaac, and the God of Jacob.' He is the God of the living, not of the dead."

33 When the crowds heard this, they were amazed at his teaching.

The Great Commandment
(Mark 12.28–34; Luke 10.25–28)

34 When the Pharisees heard that Jesus had silenced the Sadducees, they came together, ³⁵and one of them, a teacher of the Law, tried to trap him with a question. ³⁶"Teacher," he asked, "which is the greatest commandment in the Law?"

37 Jesus answered, " 'Love the Lord your God with all your heart, with all your soul, and with all your mind.' ³⁸This is the greatest and the most important commandment. ³⁹The second most important commandment is like it: 'Love your neighbour as you love yourself.' ⁴⁰The whole Law of Moses and the teachings of the prophets depend on these two commandments."

The Question about the Messiah
(Mark 12.35–37; Luke 20.41–44)

41 When some Pharisees gathered together, Jesus asked them, ⁴²"What do you think about the Messiah? Whose descendant is he?"

"He is David's descendant," they answered.

43 "Why, then," Jesus asked, "did the Spirit inspire David to call him 'Lord'? David said,

⁴⁴'The Lord said to my Lord:
    Sit here on my right
    until I put your enemies under your
        feet.'

⁴⁵If, then, David called him 'Lord,' how

22.13: Mt 8.12, 25.30; Lk 13.28   **22.23:** Acts 23.8   **22.24:** Deut 25.5   **22.32:** Ex 3.6
22.35–40: Lk 10.25–28   **22.37:** Deut 6.5   **22.39:** Lev 19.18   **22.44:** Ps 110.1

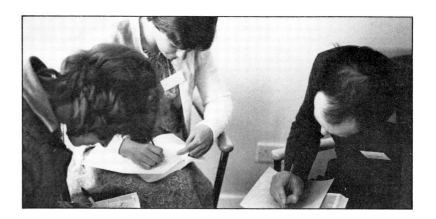

4. Using these cross-references, find the Matthew 22.37 verse in the book of Deuteronomy. Then find it in Mark and Luke. Also, find Matthew 22.39 in Leviticus.
5. Use the following worksheet.

Spend a few minutes comparing the same passage in Matthew, Mark, and Luke by answering the following questions:
a. Who asks Jesus the questions?
b. Why is Jesus asked the question?
c. What is Jesus' response to the question?
d. How does the questioner respond to Jesus?
e. What else happened?

Notice that there are some differences between the three Gospels in terms of some of the details. However, the truth of the message is the same.

Activity Six: Bible Dictionary
1. Each participant, or pair of participants, should have a copy of a Bible Dictionary to use for the following activities. See Bibliography for suggestions of some helpful Bible Dictionaries.
2. The Bible Dictionary gives more than definitions. Look at the word **covenant**. The Dictionary includes a description of how the word is used in the Bible, plus some biblical references.
3. Use the following worksheet.

Use the Bible Dictionary to find answers to some of the following questions. Each person, or pair, can choose which questions to answer. Work on as many questions as interest you or as you have time for in ten minutes.

Some Questions*

a. What is the difference between the two words **apostle** and **disciple**?

b. What is the other name for **Mount Sinai**? Where is the mountain situated?

c. Who was **Eutychus**? Why is he remembered?

d. What does the name **Ezekiel** mean?

e. Who were the **Sadducees** and the **Pharisees**?

f. What is a **parable**?

g. What does the word **gospel** mean?

* These questions are just examples of the types of questions that could be asked. The leader should prepare his or her own list of questions.

4. After spending ten minutes searching for answers to the questions, people can share what they have discovered and also share their feelings about their experiences of using Bible Concordances, parallel references and footnotes and Dictionaries.

Activity Seven: Bible Scavenger Hunt

Now that participants in the class have become familiar with some of the basic tools for Bible study, it is possible to reinforce those skills and have some fun by playing a Bible Scavenger Hunt.

The leader may want to reorganize the participants into different groupings. Each group should include five people.

1. One way to achieve this would be to select the six youngest people in the class (assuming a class of thirty people).

Each of these "youngest children" select an older "brother" or "sister". The older "brother" or "sister" choose a "mother" or "father" for their group. The "mother" or "father" chooses another member of the "family".

The "temporary families" will work together on the Scavenger Hunt. This regrouping gives people a chance to work with others apart from their own family.

2. Allow twenty minutes for the Scavenger Hunt. Give each participant a worksheet which lists all the items. The leader may want to change, add, or substitute items on the worksheet. Use any or all of the tools available for finding information.

3. After spending twenty minutes searching, announce that "Time is up." Check to see which group has the most right answers. Compare all the answers. Be sure each person ends up with a worksheet filled out with all the right answers. Spend some time discussing any questions that arise.

Bible Scavenger Hunt

1. Find Deuteronomy 6.5. List three places in the New Testament where this verse is quoted.

_____   _____   _____

2. Find the shortest _____ and the longest _____ psalms.

3. Find two places in the Old Testament where the Ten Commandments are listed.

_____   _____

4. Name a book in the Bible which represents each of the following kinds of writing:

Law _____   Prophecy _____

Poetry _____   Gospel _____

History _____   Letter _____

5. List the names of all twelve disciples (apostles).

_____   _____   _____   _____

_____   _____   _____   _____

_____   _____   _____   _____

6. Write ten important facts about a person of your own choice in the Bible.

_____   _____

_____   _____

_____   _____

_____   _____

_____   _____

7. State the original occupations of the following Bible characters:

Moses _____   Jesus _____

Amos _____   Matthew _____

Peter _____   Paul _____

8. Estimate the approximate mileage between:

Ur and Haran _____ miles

Haran and Bethel _____ miles

Land of Goshen and Mount Sinai _____ miles

Nazareth and Bethlehem _____ miles

Jerusalem and Corinth _____ miles

9. Name six bodies of water mentioned in the Bible

_____   _____   _____

_____   _____   _____

10. Place the following events in chronological order:
____ Baptism of Jesus
____ Call of Abraham
____ Preaching of Jeremiah
____ Resurrection of Jesus
____ Execution of John the Baptist
____ David anointed King of Israel
____ Captivity in Babylon
____ Day of Pentecost
____ Creation
____ Feeding of the 5,000
____ Captivity in Egypt
____ Call of Moses
____ Paul in Rome

Answers for the Scavenger Hunt
1. Matthew 22.37, Mark 12.30, Luke 10.27
2. Psalms 117 and 119
3. Exodus 20.1-17 and Deuteronomy 5.6-21

4. Law: Numbers and others
Poetry: Psalms and others
History: Acts and others
Prophecy: Isaiah and others
Gospel: Matthew, Mark, Luke and John
Letter: Romans and others
5. Simon Peter, Andrew, James son of Zebedee, John, Philip, Bartholomew, Thomas, Matthew (or Levi), James son of Alphaeus, Thaddaeus, Simon the Patriot, and Judas Iscariot (from Matthew 10.2-4)
6. Check the list of facts with a Bible Dictionary or other resource.
7. Moses: shepherd
Amos: shepherd and dresser of sycamore trees
Peter: fisherman
Jesus: carpenter
Matthew: tax collector
Paul: tentmaker
8. Use the mileage scale on a map in the atlas to check your estimates
9. Possible correct answers (and there are others)

Dead Sea	Sea of Galilee	Euphrates River
Jordan River	Red Sea	The Great Sea
Sea of Reeds	Mediterranean Sea	
Nile River	Tigris River	

10. Creation, Call of Abraham, Captivity in Egypt, Call of Moses, David anointed King, Preaching of Jeremiah, Captivity in Babylon, Baptism of Jesus, Execution of John the Baptist, Feeding of 5,000, Resurrection of Jesus, Day of Pentecost, Paul in Rome.

Unit 2: Exploring Bible Characters

A. Introduction

After people have developed some basic Bible study skills it is possible for them to engage in a process of exploring some of the interesting and important information about key people in the Bible.

It is one thing to learn about people who lived long ago; it is quite a different experience to identify with a biblical character. The activities in this unit are designed to help people identify with the circumstances and characteristics of Bible personalities.

This unit of study could involve any number of participants. It is planned for the unit to take two or three sessions of one hour each. By involving a small group of participants in the exploration of two or more Bible characters the unit could be extended to four to five sessions. Also, this unit could be completed in one session of two or three hours.

B. Unit objectives

At the end of this unit participants should be able to:

○ Use Bible resource books to find important information about one character in the Bible.

○ Relate one biblical character to others who appear before and after.

○ Identify in a personal way with some of the qualities, characteristics and circumstances of a biblical character.

○ Express in a creative way their interpretation of the importance of a key biblical character.

C. Materials needed

○ Bibles
○ Bible resource books
○ Paper and pencils
○ Name tags with names of Bible characters
○ Slide-making materials and slide projector.

D. Sequence of activities

Preparation for teaching activities

This unit can focus on either Old Testament or New Testament people. Or the leader could plan for two sessions on Old Testament people followed by two sessions on New Testament people. A fifth session could be planned to present all the visual creations of the participants.

Possible Old Testament characters

Rebecca	Amos	Josiah
Ezekiel	Gideon	Ezra
Aaron	Saul	Samuel
Jezebel	Jeremiah	David
Miriam	Isaac	Solomon
Joshua	Sarah	Nehemiah
Hosea	Absalom	Jonathan
Deborah	Moses	Joseph
Isaiah	Jacob	Abraham
Rachel	Elijah	Esau

Possible New Testament characters

Andrew	Titus	Nicodemus
Judas Iscariot	Jesus	Peter
James (son of Zebedee)	Philip (the Apostle)	Timothy
Mary Magdalene	James (brother of Jesus)	Barnabas
Paul	John the Baptist	Luke
Matthew	Mary (mother of Jesus)	Stephen
Thomas	John Mark	

Prepare name tags representing the Bible characters (self adhesive labels work well) for the participants to select and wear for the duration of the class period.

Activity one: Select a name of a Bible character
1. All the names of the Bible characters that are to be used should be displayed so that the participants can see all the names and decide which one to choose.
2. Each person selects a name and receives the name tag of that Bible character.

Activity two: Search for information
1. The following instructions should be printed and visible for all participants to refer to during their searching.

Instructions
Spend about fifteen minutes. Use whatever resources you choose in order to find answers to the following three questions:
1. What are some interesting and important bits of information about your person?
2. Who are some other important people in your character's life?
3. Between what dates did your character live? (It's not necessary to be absolutely accurate.)

There should be a variety of books and other resources available that will help people of all ages and levels of reading ability.
2. After everyone has had about fifteen minutes to work, check to see how they are doing. Encourage everyone to try to find an approximate date for their character so that they will be successful in a later activity. The leader could guide some of the participants directly to a time-line.

Activity three: Introducing the Bible characters in a time-line
When everyone has a date and some information they are ready for the next instructions.
1. Everyone write a sentence or two to introduce your character to the others. Write the introduction in the first person as if you are the person telling somebody else something about yourself.
2. After a few minutes of writing a brief introduction, the participants can be instructed to form themselves in a time-line where the Bible characters are arranged in chronological order. Where there are large gaps of time between one Bible character and another that time can be represented by empty space in the time-line.
3. Each person in turn, starting with the earliest, introduces himself or

herself in the role of the Bible person. The time-line should be in the shape of a shallow semi-circle so that everyone can see the others.

4. At the conclusion of the introductions the leader could guide a brief discussion beginning with questions like:

○ What impressions do you have about this whole group of Bible characters?

○ What things made these characters special and memorable?

○ If you could meet one of these people which one would you choose to meet? Why?

Activity four: Creative expression with slides and captions

Each participant has some basic information about at least one Bible character. Using that information it is possible to create several slides to communicate something significant about the person.

There are two types of do-it-yourself slides suggested: write-on slides, and scratch slides. The leader can use these as suggested or substitute other visual expression materials to accomplish the same objective. The materials suggested may all be available locally, but from several sources.

Each participant can create several slides in one or both of the following formats.

1. Write-on slides

A write-on slide is a piece of matt acetate in a 2″ x 2″ cardboard frame. Students can use projection pens or pencils to draw and write directly on the slide. The slide is ready for projection immediately. It is possible to draw or write on both sides. (One side is shiny and smooth, the other is dull and textured.) If water soluble projection pens and pencils are used the slides can be washed off with a soft, damp cloth and used again.

2. Scratch slides

Collect some exposed slides from your photographer friends. Often the end of a slide roll has been mounted so that there are several black, opaque slides. Black slides also result when the shutter is released and the lens cap has not been removed. Photographers usually throw these rejects away. By scratching with a sharp instrument on the side of the slide coated with the emulsion it is possible to scratch off the emulsion leaving a clear, transparent scratch. By scratching carefully, beautiful images can be created. These images can be coloured with projection pens or pencils to produce a very colourful slide. Drawing pins, dissecting needles, and other sharp instruments can be used as scratchers.

After participants have created their slides they should write one or two sentences as the "script" for each slide. The leader will collect the slides in the proper sequence for inserting in the slide tray to be projected. As the slides appear on the screen the one who created the slide reads the "script" he wrote for each slide.

Several words of caution:

○ The leader should practise each of the ways to create slides to be sure he or she understands all the steps.

○ Write out the instructions for each slide format so that participants can do it themselves without the leader having to show every step.

○ Allow some time for the participants to practise and experiment with one slide in the format they choose. They will be much more successful in their production if they can practise a little first.

○ Be sure you know how to operate the slide projector, have an extra bulb, and know how to change the bulb.

Have a lot of fun!

Unit 3: Jesus and His Followers

A. Introduction

This outline was designed for a three- to four-week unit with parents and children in the same group. The primary strategy of this unit is the use of Learning Centres. A Learning Centre is an area or surface set out with all the materials and resources necessary for an individual to carry out an activity. This is not the place to present all the information necessary to plan for and implement Learning Centres. However, there are a number of key factors that must be considered when involving a large group in using Learning Centres.

1. There needs to be a wide variety of Centres so that the participants can select something of interest to them and have sufficient space and resources with which to work. A good rule of thumb is approximately one centre for every three to five students.

2. All necessary resources and materials should be present in the Centre so that students don't waste time or lose interest.

3. Directions should be visible, brief, clear, and in logical sequence so that most students can do the activities in the Centre without having to be directed at each step by someone else.

4. The available centres should be of different levels — some complex and some more simple so that everyone will find something of interest to them.

5. Identify each Centre with a sign or symbol that indicates where it is and what its focus is. Students could be given a list of the Learning Centres available, identifying them by name, number, and brief description. In this way they will be able to make a quicker, more effective choice.

6. It is important to remember that it doesn't matter if by the end of the unit some participants will have used all the centres and others only one or two.

7. In some Centres younger students will need to be helped by the older ones, and in other Centres the younger students will be able to help the older ones.

If I were doing the planning, I would not use a unit with Learning Centres as the first experience for an intergenerational group that has not been together before. Leaders and participants will be more successful with Learning Centres if they have had the opportunity to get to know each other by working, playing and worshipping together prior to this unit.

We have outlined enough centres in the following pages to involve a group of 40 to 50 people for three to four weeks. One of the problems of using Learning Centres is that everyone "does his own thing" so there is not so much sharing and interacting with the whole group. The leader may want to plan for time at the end of each session, or even a whole session at the end of the unit, where the participants will have the opportunity to share and learn from each other. This can take the form of displays, presentations, or a programme of "show and tell".

B. Unit objectives
Each Learning Centre has one or more objectives associated with it. In this unit you will find the objectives at the beginning of the description of each Centre.

C. Materials needed
Instead of making a list here of all the materials needed, we will include a list of the appropriate materials with each Learning Centre.

D. Activities
1. People who followed Jesus
2. Pick-a-person
3. Jesus and stories
4. Watch a filmstrip on Peter and Jesus
5. Picturing Jesus
6. Jesus calls Matthew
7. Scripture cards and pictures
8. The Gospel of Mark
9. What difference does Jesus make?
10. Jesus' twelve disciples

The description of each Learning Centre includes:
1. Title
2. Objectives
3. Resources necessary to do the activities in the centre.
4. Instructions as they will be written for the students to follow.

1. People who followed Jesus

Objectives:
As a result of participating in this Centre, people should be able to:
a. Identify by name and give some relevant facts about three people who followed Jesus.

b. Use several Bible study resources to find answers to key questions.
c. Express in a creative way what they learnt about at least one person who followed Jesus.

Resources:
a. Instruction cards prepared with the five steps written out.
b. Worksheets for each student (see page 63).
c. Several copies of the *Good News Bible*.
d. Resource books including the following:
○ A Concordance
○ A Bible Encyclopaedia
○ A Bible Dictionary
(You should have available copies of these types of books suitable for both adults and children. See the Bibliography for recommended books.)
e. Creative activity resources including
○ Write-on slides
○ Magazine pictures, photographs, or slides
○ Poetry forms (see pages 78-79)

Instructions: (Written out and displayed so that everyone can see them.)
Step one: Select two or three of the following. These are all people who were followers of Jesus.

Nicodemus	Zacchaeus
Bartimaeus	Martha
Mary Magdalene	Jairus
Mary, Martha's sister	A leper

Write the two or three names on your worksheet.
Step two: Find a scripture passage about each of the people you have selected.
　Use the Index in the *Good News Bible* to help you to find the passages.
　Read the passages. Notice the four questions on the worksheet. Think about the questions as you read.
Step three: Look up the two or three names you selected in one or more of the following books (or in any others that are available):
○ A Concordance
○ Bible Dictionary
○ Bible Encyclopaedia
(You should have available copies of these books suitable for both adults and children. See the Bibliography for recommended books.)
　Read as much as you can find about each person you selected. Keep in mind the four questions on the worksheet.
Step four: Answer the following questions about each of the people you selected:
a. Why did Jesus and the person meet?

b. What happened to the person as a result of the meeting with Jesus?

c. What feelings do you think the person had towards Jesus?

d. Do people have similar experiences today? Can you think of any examples?

Write your answers on your worksheet.

Step five: Do one creative activity to express your ideas and feelings about one or more of the people you selected.

a. Create a series of write-on slides to illustrate the story in your own way.

b. Write down a list of questions you would ask if it were possible for you to interview the person.

c. Create a poem or express how you think the person reacted whilst with Jesus. Use one of the poetry forms available or make up your own.

Share what you create with a friend, teacher or someone else in the class.

(Sample worksheet)	Name	Name	Name
Question 1. Why did Jesus and the person meet?			
Question 2. What happened to the person as a result of the meeting with Jesus?			
Question 3. What feelings do you think the person had towards Jesus?			
Question 4. Do people have similar experiences today? Can you think of any examples?			

2. Pick-a-person

Objectives:

This Centre is similar to the previous one, "People who followed Jesus". In addition to the ten people included in that Centre the leaders could add the names of some of the more familiar disciples. The difference with this Centre is that each participant picks the name of just one person to be the focus for the study.

As a result of participating in this Centre people should be able to:

a. Describe some interesting and important facts about one person who followed Jesus.

b. Use several Bible study resources to find answers to key questions.

c. Illustrate in a creative way some of their impressions and insights about that biblical character.

Resources:

a. Identification and instruction cards for the Bible people to be studied (one card for each person).

b. Resource books.

c. Necessary creative activity materials. Leaders will have to gather whatever materials are suggested on the instruction cards.

Instructions:

One large poster should be displayed in the Centre with the following instructions:

**Pick-a-person
Instructions**

1. Pick one card at a time.
2. First, read any scripture passages that are recommended.
3. Answer the questions on the card.
4. Write down the answers in your notebook.
5. For questions where you need more information, use one or more of the Bible resource books that are available on the bookshelves.
6. Do at least one of the creative activities.
7. When you have finished with it, return the Pick-a-person card to the pack of cards.
8. Share the results of your work with a teacher, parent or child.

In addition to the general instructions the leaders need to prepare an Identity and Instruction Card for each of the people to be studied. Outlined below are two sample cards. Create your own questions and creative activities for the people you want the participants to study.

(Sample only)
Nicodemus
First read three passages in the Gospel of John:
John 3.1-17; 7.45-52; and 19.38-42.

Some questions
1. What kind of person was Nicodemus?
2. How do you think he felt towards Jesus?
3. Why do you suppose Nicodemus came to Jesus?
4. What feelings did Jesus seem to have towards Nicodemus?
5. What do you think might have happened to Nicodemus after Jesus had gone?

Some activities (Select one)
1. Write a list of questions to ask Nicodemus in an interview. Get someone to ask you the questions as if you are Nicodemus. Record the interview.
2. Select a painting activity to illustrate the relationship between Jesus and Nicodemus.
3. Dress up as Nicodemus and pose for a photograph, preferably an instant one.

(Sample only)
Matthew
First look up the name Matthew in the Index of the *Good News Bible*. Read all the suggested references.

Some questions
1. What kind of person was Matthew?
2. Why do you think Jesus wanted Matthew to be one of his disciples?
3. Think of some reasons why Matthew did not want to be a disciple. Think of some reasons why he would want to be one.
4. How do you think other people felt about Matthew being a disciple?
5. What thoughts might you have had about Matthew if you had been one of Jesus' other disciples?

Some activities (Select one)
1. Write out a brief conversation between two tax collectors talking about Matthew.
2. Create two drawings of Matthew, one as a tax collector, the other as a disciple.
3. Select or create slides to illustrate some important things about Matthew.

3. Jesus and stories

Objectives:
As a result of participating in this Centre people should be able to:
a. Recall several stories about Jesus or stories that Jesus told.
b. Find several of the stories in the Bible.
c. Ask several questions about one story.
d. Communicate, creatively, one story with the others in the group.

Resources:
a. A collection of stories about, and told by, Jesus. One good source is the Bible Society. We distribute a number of pamphlets – scripture portions – for new readers. See the Bibliography for our address.
b. Several different translations of the New Testament.
c. Paper and pencils.

Instructions:
In the envelope are ten stories. Some are stories about Jesus. Others are stories that Jesus told.
   Read several of the stories.
   Choose one of the stories and do the following:
a. Find the story in the Bible.
b. Read the story in another translation of the Bible.
c. Write down a list of three or more questions that come to your mind when you think about Jesus and the story.
d. Share and discuss your questions with a teacher or another student.
e. Decide on a way to illustrate your story to share it with the others in the group.

4. Watch a filmstrip on Peter and Jesus.

Objectives:
As a result of participating in the Centre people should be able to:
a. Describe some of the important impressions people had of Jesus.
b. Use the Bible and other resources to find key passages about Jesus and Peter.
c. Express in a creative way their own personal impressions of Jesus and Peter.

Resources:
a. The filmstrip "Simon called Peter" from Church Army Filmstrips. You might find that you want to re-write the script before using it. (Cat. No. VE9) You could also put a sequence about Peter together from Bible Society's Jesus of Nazareth slides.
b. Filmstrip projector or viewer, record player and screen.
c. Bibles, resource books, paper and pencils.
d. Cinquain and Diamonte poetry forms (see pages 78-79).

Instructions:
Step one Use filmstrip viewer and record player. Practise with the equipment first to be sure you can operate it.
Step two Watch the filmstrip and listen to the recording.
Step three As you watch the filmstrip think about the things you are discovering about Jesus and Peter.
Step four After watching the filmstrip make two lists of statements to complete sentences that begin:

Jesus is...	Peter is...
a.	a.
b.	b.
c.	c.
d.	d.

Step five Write a Cinquain or Diamonte Poem to express some of your thoughts and feelings about Jesus or Peter.

5. Picturing Jesus

Objectives:
As a result of participating in this Centre people should be able to:
a. Identify with one or more visual images of Jesus.
b. Explain why they selected one or more pictures of Jesus as the way they "see" Jesus.
c. Create their own picture of Jesus.

Resources:
a. A collection of teaching pictures, art reprints and other portraits of Jesus.
b. Display board, drawing pins, paper and felt pens.
c. Materials for drawing and painting.

Instructions:

Step one: Browse through all the pictures of Jesus looking for the ones you like the best.

Step two: Compare the pictures of Jesus that you like in order to select one or two pictures that you think portray Jesus most effectively.

Step three: Mount the picture you like the most on the display board.

Step four: Decide on a title or a caption to accompany your picture and write that title or caption on a card to place next to the picture.

Step five: Select whatever materials you prefer with which to create your own picture of Jesus.

Step six: Mount your picture next to the other one you selected and write a different title or caption for your picture or use the title or caption you prepared previously.

6. Jesus calls Matthew

Objectives

As a result of participating in this Centre people should be able to:

a. State some interesting and important facts about Matthew.

b. Describe some of the conflict Matthew must have encountered and felt personally as a result of becoming a disciple.

c. Express creatively some feelings or impressions about Matthew.

Resources:

a. *Good News Bible* on cassette (Matthew) or other cassettes that tell the story of Matthew's call to be a disciple.

b. Cassette recorder.

c. Materials for whatever creative activities are planned.

Instructions:

Step one: Listen to the cassette recording about Jesus calling Matthew to become a disciple.

Listen for answers to four questions:

1. What kind of man was Matthew?
2. Why do you think Jesus wanted Matthew to be a disciple?
3. What reactions did others have to Matthew being chosen as a disciple?
4. What changes did Jesus make in Matthew's life?

Step two: Find and read the story of Jesus' call to Matthew in the Bible.

Step three: Complete one of the following activities:

a. Create a set of slides to illustrate the story.

b. Write a newspaper reporter's account of the event.

c. Tape record a news report of the event.

Step four: Share with others what you have created.

7. Scripture cards and pictures

Objectives:

As a result of participating in this Centre people should be able to:

a. Use visual images of the life and work of Jesus to make a presentation of what they believe is important.

b. Select contemporary visuals to express their ideas and feelings about the life and work of Jesus.

Resources:

a. Scripture cards. These can be made by cutting line drawings from the *Good News Bible* and mounting them on 4" x 6" cards. The scripture text could be printed on the back of each card. (See *Using the Bible in Teaching,* chapter 5.)

b. A collection of photographs clipped from magazines or a stack of magazines.

c. Paper, pencils, magazines, glue, scissors and paper.

Instructions:

Step one: Browse through the pack of scripture cards. Just get acquainted with them and enjoy them.

Step two: Select as many cards as you would like. Arrange these selected cards in a sequence that communicates a message about Jesus and his followers.

Step three: Write your own captions or titles for the cards you have selected.

Step four: Select pictures from the picture collection or from magazines that will illustrate in a contemporary way a similar message as the one you created with the scripture cards.

or

Use one or more scripture cards as the central focus for creating a montage of your message. Use magazine pictures and word clippings to create your montage.

8. The Gospel of Mark

Objectives:

As a result of participating in this Centre people should be able to:

a. State some important facts about the Gospel of Mark as a whole.

b. Recall a number of the miracles Jesus performed as recorded in the Gospel of Mark.

c. Cite some examples of how Jesus responded to people and how they reacted to him.

Resources:

a. *Good News Bibles*

b. Bible resource books

c. Copies of ''Notes on the Gospel of Mark'' (This is a one page summary of notes from several sources, which the leaders should have prepared beforehand.)

d. Paper and pencils

e. Cassette tape of Mark chapters 1 – 3, and cassette recorder. (Leader can record the reading ahead of time, or use the Good News Bible on cassette.)

Instructions:

Step one: Read the ''Notes on the Gospel of Mark'' and do some research in the Bible resource books in order to answer the following questions.

a. Who was the author of the Gospel of Mark?

b. Why was the Gospel of Mark written?

c. What are some important characteristics of the Gospel of Mark?

Step two: Listen to the cassette recording of the first three chapters of the Gospel of Mark. As you are listening make a list of statements that all start with ''Jesus is ...'' Stop the recorder each time you have something to write.

Step three: Do one of the following activities:

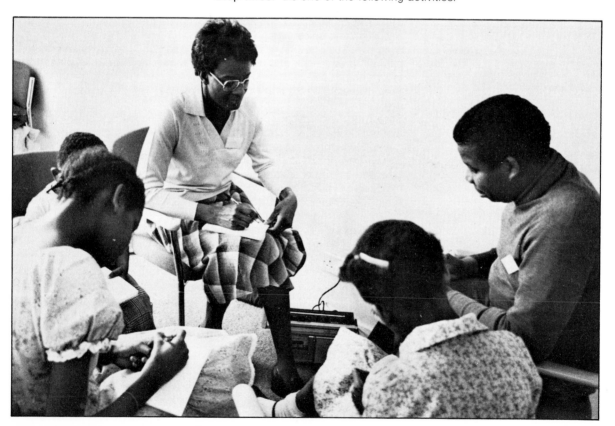

a. Skim through as many chapters of Mark as you can, looking for all the names or titles of Jesus. After you have a list, select one name or title to do some further research on and then create your own symbol to represent that name or title.

or

b. Skim through as many chapters of Mark as you can, looking for all the miracles performed by Jesus. Make a list of them and answer two questions for as many miracles as possible.

○ Why did Jesus perform the miracle?
○ What happened after the miracle?

or

c. Look for actions of Jesus and reactions of the people to Jesus in the Gospel of Mark. Make two columns:

Jesus acted by...	The people reacted to Jesus by...
_____	_____
_____	_____
_____	_____
_____	_____

9. What difference does Jesus make?

Objectives:
As a result of participating in this Centre people should be able to:
a. Describe the differences between the "before" and "after" circumstances of people who experienced meeting Jesus personally.
b. Suggest some ways that Jesus can make a difference in people's lives today.

Resources:
a. Nine specific scripture cards which could include:
1. Jesus heals ten lepers
2. Jesus calls four fishermen
3. Jesus joins Zacchaeus for dinner
4. Jesus calms a storm
5. The feeding of the 5,000
6. Jesus visits Martha and Mary
7. Jesus forgives and heals a man lowered through the roof
8. Jesus encounters Thomas
9. The miraculous conversion of Saul
b. Materials necessary for whatever creative activities are planned by the leader.

Instructions:
Step one: There are nine scripture cards. Each one represents an encounter Jesus had with other people. Look at all the scripture cards.
Step two: Choose two or three cards that interest you. Read the scripture on the back of the card. Think about the differences or changes Jesus made in the lives of the people.
Step three: Complete one of the following activities:
a. Write your own "before" and "after" stories of the people with Jesus.
or
b. Draw on paper, slides or transparencies "before" and "after" interpretations of the people with Jesus.
or
c. Conduct an interview with another person taking the roles of a reporter and a person who was helped by Jesus. Talk about the changes that happened in the person's life after he or she met Jesus.

10. Jesus' twelve disciples

Objectives:
As a result of participating in this Centre people should be able to:
a. Find at least one place in the New Testament where the twelve disciples are listed.
b. Identify by name and two facts, six of the twelve disciples.
c. Given a list of twenty names of New Testament people, identify all twelve disciples.
d. State in their own words a definition of "disciple".

Resources:
a. *Good News Bibles*
b. Bible resource books
c. A game, puzzle and test focusing on the twelve disciples.

Instructions:
Who were the twelve disciples Jesus chose?
Step one: Use either of the following two books:
○ Bible Encyclopaedia
○ Dictionary of the Bible
Look up the word "disciple" and read the definition. (You should have books available that are suitable for children and adults.)
Step two: Complete the sentence in your own words:

A disciple is _____

_____

_____

Step three: Find at least one place in the New Testament where the twelve disciples are listed. Use Bible reference books and the Index in the *Good News Bible* to do this.
Hint: Look under the word "apostle" also.

The twelve disciples (apostles) were:

1.	2.
3.	4.
5.	6.
7.	8.
9.	10.
11.	12.

Step four: To find out more about the disciples or to help you remember their names you can choose to do one of the following fun things.
a. A crossword puzzle.
b. Play a game of cards, such as Disciple Rummy.
c. See a filmstrip.

Sample activities for some learning centres
Here are some examples of games, puzzles and forms that could be used in some of the learning centres. We suggest that leaders use these as samples to give them ideas of things they can make up to fit their particular situation rather than use them as they stand.

A. Crossword puzzles on the apostles
1. The Apostles
Down
1. Was a tax collector when Jesus called him. (Matthew 9.9)
2. Known as "the doubter". (John 20.24-29)
3. Name changed from Simon to _____which means "rock".
(Matthew 16.13-20)
5. The one elected to take Judas' place.(Acts 1.21-26)
6. Not one of the original twelve apostles, but identified as an apostle and author of many letters in the New Testament. (Romans 1.1)
11. Known as a zealot. (Matthew 10.4)
14. The one who betrayed Jesus for thirty coins (Matthew 26.14-16)

Across
4. A lesser known apostle, mentioned with Philip. (Matthew 10.3)
7. A fisherman from Capernaum and brother of Peter. (Matthew 4.18-20)
8. A lesser known apostle, also called Judas son of James. (Matthew 10.3 and Luke 6.16)
9. The apostle who brought Nathaniel to Jesus. (John 1.43-46)

10. A son of Zebedee. (Matthew 4.21-22)
12. A son of Alphaeus. (Matthew 10.3)
13. A fisherman, one of the inner circle of disciples closest to Jesus. (Matthew 17.1)

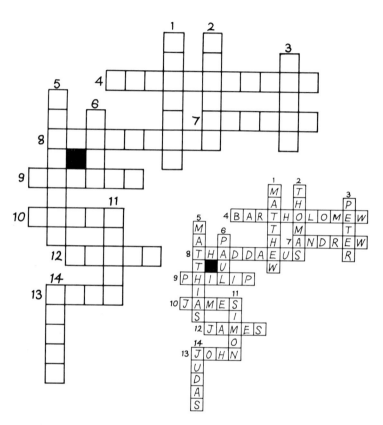

2. Peter, the Apostle

Down

1. Peter's work before he became a disciple.
2. When asked at Jesus' trial if he knew Jesus, Peter _____ knowing him.
3. Peter _____ that Jesus was God's Messiah.
5. The garden where Jesus prayed and the disciples slept before Jesus' arrest.
6. On the day of Pentecost, Peter _____ to many people.
9. The word from the Greek that means ''Messiah''.

11. The one to whom Peter said, "You are the Christ, the Son of the living God."
13. Peter's brother.

Across
4. A Jewish festival fifty days after Passover.
7. A person who follows and learns from Jesus is called a _____.
8. In Greek the name Peter means _____.
10. The city where Peter spent his last days.
12. Peter _____ a lame man.
14. Peter was also called by an Aramaic name which means "rock".
15. Peter's name before Jesus changed it.
16. Peter was an important _____ of the early church.
17. Two _____ (epistles) bear Peter's name in the New Testament.
18. Peter fell when he tried to walk on _____.

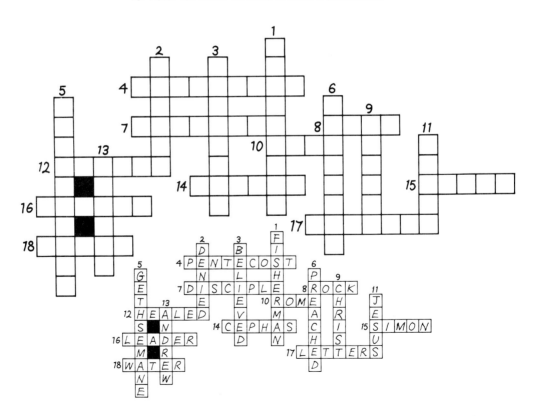

B. Three matching worksheets

Matching games can be put on photocopied sheets, magnetic boards, or flannelgraph boards.

Match Column A with the correct answer in Column B.

1. Peter, the Apostle

Column A	**Column B**
Before being called by Jesus to be a disciple, Peter was a _____	Pentecost
Peter's brother was _____.	Simon
When Jesus asked Peter, "Who do you say that I am?" Peter answered_____.	Rome
Before being named "Peter" by Jesus his name was_____.	John Mark
The name "Peter" means_____.	
(True or false) Peter was always like a "rock" in his faithfulness to Jesus.	False
A man who was a companion of Peter and author of one of the Gospels.	"You are the Christ, the Son of the living God."
The disciples were gathered in Jerusalem when they received God's Holy Spirit and Peter preached on the day of _____.	Rock
	Fisherman
The city where Peter was crucified and buried.	Andrew

2. Jesus' disciples

Column A	**Column B**
A fisherman from Capernaum and brother of Peter.	Matthias

The one who betrayed Jesus for 30 coins.	Philip
Was a tax collector when Jesus called him.	Matthew
Name changed from Simon to _____ which means "rock."	Andrew
Known as "the doubter".	Judas
The one elected to take Judas' place.	Thomas
A fisherman, one of the 12 disciples closest to Jesus.	James
Not one of the original 12 but identified as an apostle.	John
The disciple who brought Nathaniel to Jesus.	Paul
The other son of Zebedee.	Peter

3. Others who followed Jesus

Column A	Column B
A Pharisee, who asked Jesus good questions. Helped to bury Jesus.	Joseph of Arimathea
A tax collector, a small man Jesus visited in his home.	Lazarus
Jesus talked with this woman at a well about "living water" and "true worship".	Bartimaeus
Brother of Mary and Martha, Jesus brought him back to life.	Jairus
A woman follower of Jesus. Present at his crucifixion and resurrection.	Mary Magdalene

Lived in Bethany. The sister who was busy with housework.	Mary
A synagogue official whose daughter was healed by Jesus.	Zacchaeus
A blind beggar who was healed by Jesus and then became a follower.	Nicodemus
Sister of Lazarus who paid careful attention to Jesus' teaching.	Samaritan woman
A secret follower of Jesus who provided the tomb for Jesus' burial.	Martha

C. Three creative poetry forms

Cinquain Cinquain is a poetry form that has a very special style that gives it its name. The word "cinquain" refers to the number five. There are five lines in the poem. A Cinquain is usually done with these guidelines.

Line 1	Title (a noun: one word)	———
Line 2	Describes the title (two words)	——— ——— .
Line 3	Action words or phrase about the title (three words)	——— ——— ———
Line 4	Describes a feeling about the title (four words)	——— ——— ——— ———
Line 5	Refers to the title (one word)	———

Diamonte A Diamonte poem uses opposites. First choose a key word. Put it in the first line. Think of an opposite. Put this in the last line. Follow the directions in column A and put your response on the line with the same number in column B. The middle line (7) is a summary line that brings both opposites together.

Column A	Column B
1. Noun.	1._____
2. Noun which is opposite or contrast to the noun used on line 1.	3._____ _____
3. Two words that describe the noun on line 1.	5._____ _____ _____
4. Two words that describe the noun on line 2.	7._____
5. Three "-ing words" that are action words related to the noun on line 1.	6._____ _____ _____
6. Three "-ing words" that are action words related to the noun on line 2.	4._____ _____
7. A phrase that unites both the nouns (line 1 and line 2)	2._____

Haiku The Haiku is a poetry form that has come to us from Japan. Traditionally Haiku are written about some aspect of the natural world and the seasons of the year. We are using the Haiku form for our purposes, and the experiences and feelings expressed are not limited by specific subject matter.

Haiku consist of three, unrhymed, unmetered lines, with five syllables in the first line, seven in the second, five in the third, making seventeen syllables in all.

The Haiku is not expected to make a complete statement. Through its seventeen concentrated syllables, it has the power to evoke associations, images, and feelings in a listener or a reader.

_____ _____ _____ _____ _____
_____ _____ _____ _____ _____ _____ _____
_____ _____ _____ _____ _____

D. Blank playing cards

Many games can be made up to teach biblical facts by using a set of blank cards and permanent ink pens.

Here are instructions for a game that we made up called Disciple Rummy:

Disciple Rummy Rules In the pack of cards are the names of Jesus' disciples and names of other people in the Old and New Testament.

Each name has three cards.

The object of the game is to "meld" as many pairs of cards as possible.

You may meld when you have two cards with the same name on them.

To play

Deal 7 cards.

Put left-over cards in the centre of the table face down. This pile becomes the "draw".

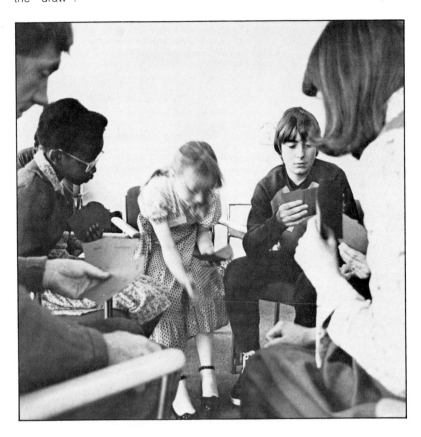

Each person has a turn in which he:
○ Draws one card from the top of the deck to add to his hand.
○ Melds any pairs of names (face up on the table).
○ Discards one card face up.

A player may pick up the pile of discarded cards instead of taking a card from the "draw" if he has one card in his hand that matches the top card on the discard pile. If he does this he must meld the top card and he must take all the cards in the discard pile. Cards already melded cannot be used when picking up the discard pile.

Meld must be put down only when it is your turn and before you discard.

Once you meld you cannot return the cards to your hand.

The game is over when there are no more cards in the draw pile, or when someone is out (has no cards left in his hand).

When the game ends count your points:
○ 5 points for each pair of disciples
○ 2 points for each other pair of names
○ Bonus of 2 points for each set of three matching cards
○ Penalty of 2 points for each card left in your hand when the game ends.

Unit 4: Family Bible Study

A. Introduction

A distinctive feature, and challenge, of this programme was that all groups were meeting outside on the lawns and among the trees. With over one hundred small groups, meeting outside, we were limited as to the kinds and quantities of equipment and resources we could use. In order to involve all age groups in creative ways it was important to have some resources available. We solved this problem by producing a cassette tape with instructions, scripture readings, songs, and stories. Two co-leaders were allotted to each team and they brought their own cassette recorder. In addition to the cassette tape for leaders to share with their groups, each family was provided with a "creativity sack". Each creativity sack was filled with: a piece of burlap, scraps of felt, magazine, scripture cards, construction paper, poetry forms, message notes with envelopes, and printed sheets with suggestions for meditation. The leaders were also provided with some scissors, bottles of glue, pencils, extra paper, magazines and felt.

From reports received from many leaders and participants it seems that most people enjoyed the Bible study, had positive feelings about doing the study as groups of families, and learned much in the process.

B. Unit objectives

At the end of this unit, people and their families, will be enabled to:
○ Identify some of the feelings of conflict and celebration experienced in their families.

○ Relate three Bible stories to experiences in their own families.
○ Set some goals to accomplish in their families.
○ Reflect on some of their important family traditions.
○ Respond to the needs of other people in their families and neighbourhoods.

C. Materials needed
The materials needed are identified specifically in each session.

D. Sequence of activities

First session – Conflict

After a time for getting acquainted and setting the stage the whole group will be ready for the first activity.

Activity one: The parable of the lost son
1. The leader could introduce the parable with something like the following statement:

> Jesus told stories to help people understand some important things about relationships with God and between people. These stories Jesus told are known as parables. A parable is a way of using common, ordinary things that people know about to help explain some other ideas about God that are harder to understand. Today we are going to focus on a parable Jesus told about a father and two sons. One son stays at home and helps his father, while the other son takes what belongs to him and goes away to a city where he spends all his money.

2. Before reading the parable, organize the large group into three smaller groups. Each small group will identify with one of the main characters in the story. It is best for people to decide for themselves (even the younger children) which characters they will focus their interest on. However, it is also important that the three groups are fairly evenly divided. Perhaps some will focus on their "second choice" to help even-up the groups. This dividing of the group can be accomplished with instructions such as:

> Each of us is going to hear this parable from the point of view of one of the people in the story. We are going to try to think and feel like one of the characters. We need some people to be fathers, some others to be sons who stayed at home, and others to be sons who went away from home. Choose the one you want to be.

3. After checking to see that everyone has made a choice and to see the "spread" of the choices, give one last instruction before reading the parable:

As you listen to this parable put yourself in the place of the person you chose. Think about all the feelings and thoughts your person might have had.

4. Read the Parable of the Lost Son (Luke 15.11-32). Someone can read while others listen or the others can follow along in their own Bibles. Or reading could be recorded on cassette tape by someone who can be a little more dramatic with the reading. Or the parable can be presented visually as well as verbally with a filmstrip. The filmstrip "Lost and Found" part two, available from the Church Army, could be used frames 8-17 (Cat. No. HP79).

Activity two: Meet in the three small groups
The three groups are organized according to the three people in the parable so that all the fathers will meet together; likewise with the two sons. (If the small groups have eight or more people in them, then divide the groups up so that they will be smaller.) In these small groups make a list of all the feelings and thoughts the person might have had and discuss the reasons for those feelings and thoughts. Allow about seven to ten minutes for this smaller group discussion.

Activity three: Family discussions
1. Regroup and meet in small "family" groups composed of one or two of each of the three people. There will be many "family" groups all discussing among themselves simultaneously.
2. Each person will speak to others from the point of view of his person (father, or one of the two sons) focusing on two questions:
○ How do you feel about yourself and what happened to you?
○ How do you feel about the other two people?
People should share their feelings and thoughts as clearly and briefly as possible. And they should listen to what others have to share.

Activity four: Large group reflection and discussion
The group leader(s) can guide the discussion using some of the following questions as guidelines:
○ What were some of the conflicts in the story?
○ How were the conflicts resolved?
○ Are there conflicts like these in our own families?
○ How can we resolve or learn to live with our conflicts?
○ What is the main point or message of the parable?
○ What things do you think Jesus was trying to help us discover about ourselves?

Activity five: Creative expression
There are a variety of possible activities through which people can express

themselves creatively in order to convey to others their understanding of the parable and its meaning for their lives today. Possible creative activities include:

O Writing a Cinquain poem
O Writing a Haiku poem
O Selecting magazine pictures and captions to illustrate the feelings of the people in the parable, or perhaps to illustrate a poem they or someone else has written.
O Making a montage with magazine pictures, adverts and captions.
O Paraphrasing the parable using contemporary language and situations.

After a time for creating, be sure to provide a time for people to share with others what they have created.

Second session – Acceptance

This session is designed to help people and families to identify and accept their individual uniqueness and to celebrate their acceptance by God.

After a brief time of opening, introduction, or setting the stage the following activities may be appropriate.

Activity one: Identifying the characteristics of friendship
If the group is small you can all work together on the following activity. If the group is large, you may want to divide into smaller groups of four or five people per group.

1. Identify the kinds of things people do in order to show their friendship. What makes a friend a friend? Make a list of all the ideas you have. The leader may want to give some examples to help people get started.
For example:
O When a friend asks you how you are...they really want to know!
O A friend comes to your house to play with *you*, not just to play with your toys.
O To become a friend you make a special effort to spend time with another person to get to know all about him or her.
O Sharing a meal helps people become friends.

2. When the group(s) have finished making the list, give everyone a chance to discuss the following questions:
O What are some things we can do to help people become friends?
O Are there any times you can think of when it is better not to try and become a friend to someone? Why?
O What are some things we do that keep people from wanting to be friends with us?
O What are some things we can do to be a better friend?

Activity two: sharing family traditions
1. We are all friends to each other in our families and in this group. One of

the things that makes a family very special for everyone in that family is the traditions that families create and celebrate. Families develop traditions around meals, holidays, birthdays, vacations, games, and many other family events. Let's think about and share some of our family traditions.

2. Each family spends time discussing among themselves some of their traditions. Each person in the family can share one or more of their favourite family traditions.

3. After some time of sharing within the family they should select one or two very special traditions to share with others in the larger group.

4. During the time for the large group sharing, each family can take a few minutes to share their traditions and to respond to each other.

Activity three: Focus on Zacchaeus

1. A transition is necessary between family traditions and the next activity which focuses on Zacchaeus. Some points to emphasize could be:

> We have talked about friendship and family traditions. These are the kinds of relationships and experiences that make life very special and in many ways, very Christian. Now we want to think about Jesus and some of the relationships and experiences that made him very special to other people. Zacchaeus became a friend because of his encounter with Jesus. Jesus' disciples became very special friends as a result of the experiences with him.

2. Read two different passages of scripture.

○ Luke 19.1-10 Jesus' encounter with Zacchaeus.

○ Luke 22.7-20 Jesus and his disciples' last supper.

3. Working in small groups, compare the two passages and spend some time discussing questions such as:

○ What examples are there of friendship in these two stories?

○ What similarities are there between the meal with Zacchaeus and the meal with the disciples?

○ How do we usually go about deciding who is to be invited to a special meal or to whose home we want to go for a special meal?

○ Why do you think Jesus decided to go to Zacchaeus' home? Why did he decide to have a last supper with his disciples?

Activity four: Time for meditation and creativity

1. Encourage each person to spend some time alone, or with another member of his family or a friend, in meditation which can be guided by the thoughts that are included on the page, "Something to think about." Be sure each person has a copy of this page.

2. While people are reading, thinking, and praying, it may be appropriate to have some music playing in the background.

3. After a time of meditation and reflection, encourage people to create poems, banners, posters, or collages to express some of their thoughts.

SOMETHING TO THINK ABOUT

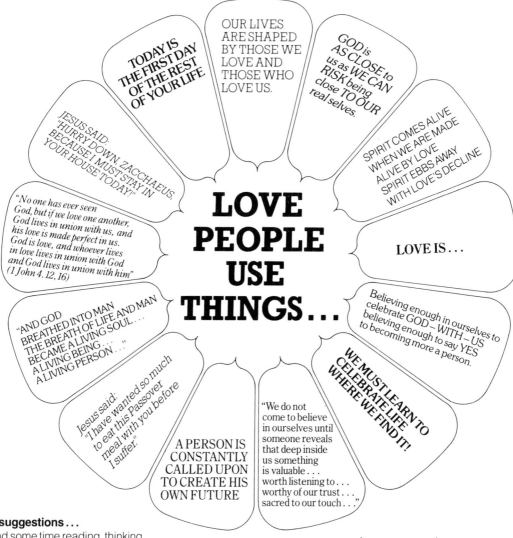

TODAY IS THE FIRST DAY OF THE REST OF YOUR LIFE

OUR LIVES ARE SHAPED BY THOSE WE LOVE AND THOSE WHO LOVE US.

GOD is AS CLOSE to us as WE CAN RISK being close TO OUR real selves.

JESUS SAID, "HURRY DOWN, ZACCHAEUS, BECAUSE I MUST STAY IN YOUR HOUSE TODAY!"

SPIRIT COMES ALIVE WHEN WE ARE MADE ALIVE BY LOVE SPIRIT EBBS AWAY WITH LOVE'S DECLINE

"No one has ever seen God, but if we love one another, God lives in union with us, and his love is made perfect in us. God is love, and whoever lives in love lives in union with God and God lives in union with him" (1 John 4. 12, 16)

LOVE PEOPLE USE THINGS . . .

LOVE IS . . .

Believing enough in ourselves to celebrate GOD – WITH – US believing enough to say YES to becoming more a person.

"AND GOD BREATHED INTO MAN THE BREATH OF LIFE AND MAN BECAME A LIVING SOUL . . . A LIVING BEING . . . A LIVING PERSON . . ."

WE MUST LEARN TO CELEBRATE LIFE WHERE WE FIND IT!

Jesus said: "I have wanted so much to eat this Passover meal with you before I suffer."

A PERSON IS CONSTANTLY CALLED UPON TO CREATE HIS OWN FUTURE

"We do not come to believe in ourselves until someone reveals that deep inside us something is valuable . . . worth listening to . . . worthy of our trust . . . sacred to our touch . . ."

Some suggestions . . .

1. Spend some time reading, thinking, and reflecting on the above statements.
2. Choose a way to express some of your feelings and ideas.
   You can do any of the following:
   – write a poem
   – decide on a word, phrase, or design from which to create a banner
   – make a poster
3. The materials could express your reponses to one of the following:

I am a person who . . .
I believe . . .
Me and my family . . .

Jesus is special because . . .
Me and my friends . . .
I want to be a person who . . .

Third session – Commitment

Activity one: The story of the Good Samaritan
1. Present the parable of the Good Samaritan to the whole class. The story can be presented by the teacher reading it, telling the story, or showing a filmstrip. The story can also be presented by having people read the story to themselves.
2. Discuss the following questions:
○ Why do you think Jesus told this story?
○ What is the point of the story?
○ Does anything like this ever happen today?

The second part of the filmstrip "Parables of Jesus" (frames 8-17) is suitable for this exercise. It is available from Church Army Filmstrips (Cat. No. HP79)

Activity two: Good Samaritans in our world.
1. Have available newspapers and magazines which tell about the good and the tragic situations which people in our society are experiencing today.
2. As individuals (if the group is small) or in small groups of three or four people, look through the newspapers and magazines to find examples of one or both of the following:
○ Contemporary "Good Samaritan" stories
○ Situations where a "good samaritan" is needed.
3. After everyone has found one or two stories, allow time for the stories to be shared. The person doing the sharing should explain to the group what connection they see between their story and the Good Samaritan story from the Bible, and why they chose this story.

Sharing can be done by *briefly* telling the story, or by presenting a creative activity the individual or group has done to communicate their story. Creative activities could include: skits, drawings, recording a cassette tape, etc.

The teacher may decide to choose the stories before class and pass them out to small groups instead of having people look for the stories themselves if the class time is short.

Activity three: Families respond to neighbours
1. People will work in family groups to make lists of people they know in their own families or comrnunities who need neighbours, friends, and the love and concern of others.
2. After a few minutes of working on their lists the families can share some of the people on their lists by telling a little about the ones they mention.
3. The leader can guide the whole group in a brief discussion of some ways it would be possible to be Jesus' kind of neighbour to these people.
4. Each family, or member of the family, can decide on one person to whom to respond with some caring and loving actions. Decisions should be made regarding specific ways they are going to relate to the people they have

identified as needing a caring neighbour. There are many possible actions which may include:
○ a phone call or note
○ an invitation for a meal
○ providing transport
○ a visit for conversation
○ helping accomplish some task the people are unable to do for themselves.

Activity four: Responding with creativity
Individuals, small groups or families could spend the remaining time of the session responding to the theme of the session with some special creativity. Possible activities include:

○ Use magazine pictures to illustrate the Parable of the Good Samaritan.
○ Write a paraphrase of the parable with familiar contemporary words and examples.
○ Use note cards to write to people in the family or community who need to hear from a friend or neighbour.
○ Create a banner or sign to proclaim a message of love and concern for other people.
○ Any other creative activities that the leaders plan.
After spending time on creative work it is important for people to have a chance to share what they have created.
    If it is appropriate, the session could be concluded by everyone standing in a circle, holding hands, and singing ''They'll know we are Christians by our love''.

Unit 5: Creation and Creativity

A. Introduction
The sessions included in this unit could be rearranged in a variety of ways. The sessions could be used as single experiences without any connection to each other. The sessions could be developed all together through the use of learning centres. Single sessions from this unit could be added to other units. Or the four sessions could be presented together in a four-week sequence.

B. Unit objectives
Each session has specific objectives which are stated as a part of the session. In addition the following objectives may be accomplished as a result of experiencing the whole unit.

At the end of this unit participants should be able to:
○ Express their own concepts of God's work as creator.
○ Describe ways that they are participants in and benefactors of God's creative work in the world.

C. Materials needed
The following materials will be needed for two or more of the sessions:
○ *Good News Bibles*
○ Bible Concordances
○ Paper, pencils, felt-tip pens
○ Creative activity materials

D. Sequence of sessions and activities

First session – Experience with light

Objectives
At the end of the session the participants should be able to:
○ Locate some passages in the Bible that emphasize the concept of light.
○ State in their own words the importance of light.
○ Illustrate in a creative way a Bible passage that focuses on light.
○ Make a connection between the physical reality of light in the world and the symbolic meaning of light as used by Jesus.

Materials needed
○ Candles and matches, blindfolds, flashlight
○ Materials for experimenting with light
○ Creative activity materials
○ Overhead projector and/or slide projector if needed

Activity one: Recall experiences with light
The group can start all together, or in small groups (not necessarily family

groups), by having each person share any experiences he or she can recall where light was of significance. (Sunburn, lost in the dark, lights, candles etc.)

Activity two: Light in the Bible

1. The leader could make a transition from personal experiences involving light to a biblical focus on light by including some of the following ideas:

○ Light is important. We have no life without light. In the creation story we read, "Then God commanded, 'Let there be light'—and light appeared. God was pleased with what he saw."

○ Jesus said, "I am the light of the world. Whoever follows me will have the light of life and will never walk in darkness."

It is also true that we have no life without *the Light*. We are going to find out more about the place of light in the Bible.

2. Either the leader should locate some key passages from the Old and New Testaments which emphasize light so that the participants can select which passages to read and discuss. Or participants could use a Concordance to find their own passages to study and discuss. Or the leader could plan for a combination of the two activities listed above.

3. Some questions to think about when reading the Bible passages, and to discuss later, could include:

○ Does the reference to light imply a physical reality or a symbolic meaning?

○ What is the meaning of light in the passage?

○ What are the characteristics of light?

○ What are the sources and uses of light?

Activity three: Two alternative activities

Select one of the following activities, or proceed to Activity Four if you prefer.

○ Ask a school teacher or other person who has experience with and interest in some aspects of light to guide the group in some experiences of or experiments with light. Use lenses or prisms. View through a telescope. Use light sensitive paper or film with which to create.

○ Invite a blind person as a guest with whom the group could discuss his or her concept and experience of light. In what way is the reality and symbolism of light important to a person who is blind?

Activity four: A blindfolded "trust walk"

1. Get everyone to choose a partner whom they trust. Give one blindfold to each pair.

2. Spend 30 minutes or so letting the pairs take each other on "trust walks". This is especially effective if done other than in the classroom. A playground

is a good place. Thirty minutes may not be enough time if the students really get involved.

3. If you want to extend the time add a meal to the experience. Eating with a blindfold on really makes us aware of how much we depend upon and take for granted our ability to see.

4. When you return to the room discuss the experience.

○ How did you feel about not being able to see?

○ About the person who was leading you?

○ About leading the other person?

Activity five: Celebrate light

1. Darken the room or go to a room that can be darkened. Sit silently in the dark. Spend a few moments thinking about all the previous experiences of light and dark.

2. Leader lights one candle and reads from the Gospel of John where Jesus says, "I am the light of the world. Whoever follows me will have the light of life and will never walk in darkness."

3. Allow a few moments of meditation and reflection.

4. Without a word being spoken the leader can direct a flashlight to some pictures mounted on the wall or to some important objects in the room.

5. If each person has a candle, the leader can quote from Matthew 5.14-16 where Jesus said, "You are like light for the whole world..." while he or she lights his or her own candle and then passes the light on to others so they can light their candles.

6. While everyone holds his lighted candle a hymn can be sung and a prayer or prayers spoken to conclude the Celebration of Light.

Second session – Experiences with colour

Objectives

At the end of the session the participants should be able to:

○ Identify some associations of meaning or experience with a variety of colours.

○ Use colours in creative ways to express feelings, messages or a story.

Materials needed

○ Books about colour or which use a lot of colours
○ Bibles
○ Finger paints and paper
○ Crayons or coloured chalks and paper
○ Tape recorder or record player
○ Overhead projector
○ Clock crystal or clear shallow bowl
○ Food colouring, oil and water
○ Kaleidoscope and cellophane

A few words about colour

We live in a world of colours. Colours surround us in colourful clothes, colour television, colours by the dozens. Colours communicate feelings. People respond to colours in various ways. Colours are used as symbols on church vestments. Part of the process of communicating is to learn how to use and respond to colours. There are many ways in which emphasis on colour can enhance teaching activities in the church. In this session we plan for people to become more sensitive and aware of colours as part of God's great creation.

Activity one: Introduction to colour

1. Talk about favourite colours. Why is one colour a favourite? This sharing could be done in the large group, by family groups, or in other small groups of three or four people.

2. Guide people who select the same colour as their favourite to find each

other and share their reasons for choosing that colour.

3. Introduce the variety of resources that are available on the tables in the room to experiment with and experience colours.

Activity two: Experiences of colour

Part of the room can be set up with the following tables of resources. People can move from table to table to browse and then select one or two tables to spend more time at.

Table A

Kaleidoscopes, cellophane, coloured plastic pieces and other materials to use to experiment with colour. Some kaleidoscopes have clear glass which can be used to look at people, pictures and objects. The resulting images are exciting and beautiful.

Table B

Books about colour and other books that are colourful. (Ladybird produce lots of books that would be useful for this table.)

Table C

Record player or tape recorder with music that would be appropriate as background and to motivate people to respond to the music with finger painting.

Table D

A listening centre with tape recorder where people listen to a recording prepared by the teacher that would guide the participants to respond with colours. For example, the tape might include:

O   Short selections of various kinds of music (loud, soft, fast, slow, dreamy, marching, eerie, joyful, sad, etc.)

O   Words such as party, death, fire, lost, children, picnic, cold, wet, gentle, fight, soft, hard, etc.

O   Sounds such as a slamming door, footsteps, crying, laughter, running water, rain storm with thunder, siren, etc.

Instructions on the tape would lead people to listen and respond to what they hear with colours. Several pieces of paper should be available and a large variety of colours of crayons or chalk.

Table E

An overhead projector can be used to create a montage of colour. Use a shallow, clear bowl or, if you can secure one, the glass face of a large clock like those in schools and offices (called a clock crystal).

1. Place the bowl or clock crystal on top of the overhead projector.

2. Pour enough water in to cover the bottom of the bowl.

3. Pour into the water some lubricating oil. Let the oil form into a number of globules.

4. Squirt a few drops of food colour into the oil. Watch what happens and enjoy the colourful display. Add another colour, then another. Rock the crystal gently to see what happens.

Another way to use the same materials
1. Use two clock crystals or bowls of the same size.
2. Pour a little water in the bottom crystal, add some oil, and one colour of food colouring.
3. Place the second crystal inside the first and add some water, oil, and a second colour of food colouring.
4. By squeezing the two crystals together you are able to produce an amazing display of designs and colour.
5. With a little practice it is possible to move the crystals and colours to accompany music in a way that interprets the music.
Table F
With a slide projector and some basic materials to work with, people could create some beautiful expressions of colour. One or more of the following types of slides could be used:
○ Write-on slides
○ Opaque film scratch slides
○ Polarized slides

Activity three: Sharing our creations of colour
In family or other small groups, or in the whole group or in combinations of small groups, people can share what they have experienced and created. They can discuss whether or not they used their favourite colours, whether they discovered anything about colours, and whether they have any additional favourite colours.

Activity four: Celebrating colour
One or more of the following activities could be used to celebrate our experiences of colour.
1. Search for one or more Bible verse that uses one's favourite colour.
2. Select some songs and hymns that use colour, to sing or to listen to.
3. Prayers of thanksgiving for God's gift of colours.

Third session: Experiences with water

Objectives
At the end of the session the participants should be able to:
○ List some ways that water is important to our lives.
○ Find some passages in the Bible that emphasize both the physical reality and symbolic significance of water.
○ Express in a creative way the meaning and importance of water.

Materials needed
○ Bibles, Concordances, paper and pencils
○ Glass jug, glasses, water
○ Creative activity materials

Activity one: Memories of water
Divide the group into small groups of three or four people to share their responses to two questions:
○ What are one or two memories you have of experiences that involved water in some way?
○ What feelings do you recall having in relation to those experiences?

Activity two: Water in the Bible
1. Give each person a *Good News Bible*. Have some Concordances available, and perhaps a few Bible Dictionaries, so that participants will have some resources available to find passages where water is the central concept.
2. Each person or small group is to select one or two passages where water is the central concept.
3. Then answer two questions related to the passage(s).
○ If water, in this passage, is a physical reality does it have any other symbolic meaning?
○ If water is used symbolically what is its meaning?
4. It is helpful in mixed groups for people to work in twos and threes so that non-readers or those learning to read will have people who can help them. Each group can share with another group the passage(s) they found and their answers to the questions.
5. The leader can summarize the focus on water from the Bible by emphasizing the symbol of water used in Baptism.

Activity three: Time for creating
There are many activities that you can use so that the participants can express themselves creatively. You might like to use some of the activities that were used in previous sessions.

Activity four: Celebrate water
1. Share the creative expressions of all the participants.
2. Read one or more of the passages of scripture on water.
3. Sing a suitable song.
4. Use a large glass jug filled with cold, fresh water. Give each person a small glass. Move among the persons pouring water in each glass saying the words, ''Jesus said, 'You shall never thirst'.''
5. Close with prayer.

Unit 6: Let us Break Bread Together

A. Introduction
Through the three sessions of this unit we are trying to bring together three different emphases all focused on meals, food or bread: meals we share, Holy Communion, and world hunger.

Sharing meals is one experience that everyone in our groups will have in common, so we start by focusing on meals. Relationships that are shared at a meal are special relationships. Therefore, we want to spend time focusing on meals that people shared with Jesus to see if we can discover something about Jesus and his relationships with others.

The climax of our study of meals with Jesus will lead us further to think about a special meal Jesus shared with his faithful followers, and which we continue to celebrate at Holy Communion.

After considering breaking bread at meals with others and a Special Meal with Jesus, we realize that there are many in the world who do not have bread to eat or to share. Often these same people are not aware of Jesus as the one who said, ''I am the Bread of Life.''

This unit could be used in part to focus the group's attention in preparation for a celebration of Holy Communion. Or the unit could be

expanded, especially the part on world hunger, to be coordinated with a larger, special programme in the church that seeks to involve people in a programme of study and action related to world hunger.

B. Unit objectives

As a result of participating in this unit people should be able to:

○ Identify some memories and feelings they have that are associated with meals they have shared with other people.

○ Participate in the planning, preparing, serving and clearing up of a special meal.

○ Recall some special meals other people shared with Jesus and describe something of the importance of two or more of those meals.

○ Explain in their own words why Holy Communion is a very important celebration in the life of the church.

○ Compare some of the parts of the Communion Service with their experiences of relationships with people and with meals.

○ Identify some of the causes and examples of world poverty. What would some possible solutions be?

○ Work on a special project in the church or community that would be a Christian response to the problem of world hunger.

C. Materials needed

The following items will be used in one or more of the four sessions:

○ Food
○ Bibles
○ Paper and pencils
○ Slides
○ Poetry forms
○ Creative activity materials

D. Sequence of sessions and activities

First session – Sharing meals with others

Activity one: Family meals

1. People can meet in family groups. Each parent and each child will share some of their own memories and feelings. If there are some in the total group who are not with their families then they can join with one of the family groups. Or, if the total group is composed of a mixture of people without reference to family structure, then the group can be subdivided in any one of several ways in order to have small groups of four to five people.

2. Parents, or adults, share first. Briefly describe from their memories of childhood one or two experiences of meals shared with the family.

3. Children share after the adults. Describe one or two things they like about sharing meals with their families.

4. Another way for younger and older people to share with each other is to describe the family dinner table at the time when they were young children.

○ What room was it in?
○ How many were gathered round the table?
○ What special memories are associated with the table?

Activity two: Values associated with meals

People in the group can discuss together in two's and three's the following rank orders. There are three rank orders. Use one or more of them, or the leader can devise different ones. Be sure to give each item its own ranking. Top ranking would be "1", next would be "2", and so on. After doing the ranking, people should share with each other in the small groups their reasons for ranking the items high and low.

Rank Order 1
To eat in a restaurant would you prefer:
___ a hamburger bar
___ a pizza place
___ a steak house
___ a fancy restaurant?

Rank Order 2
To celebrate your birthday would you prefer a meal with:
___ one special person
___ your whole family
___ a large group of friends
___ a small group of friends?

Rank Order 3
Which do you like best:
___ a progressive dinner
___ a potluck supper
___ a picnic
___ dinner in a restaurant?

Activity three: Preparing a meal

After the ranking exercise, the leader needs to help the group to see the connection between the values we have regarding meals and actually planning a meal. This meal should take place sometime before the next session.

There are many elements involved, depending upon the number and ages of people and the time available. Some possibilities include:

○ salads
○ beverages
○ main dishes
○ desserts
○ room arrangement
○ table decorations
○ name tags
○ placemats
○ songs for fun and inspiration
○ prayer or grace sung before meal

○ interaction around the tables and other ideas you may have

People can volunteer for various responsibilities and then work with others to make the necessary plans for the meal.

Activity four: Sharing the meal

Second session – Meals with Jesus

Activity one: setting the stage
The last time we were together we shared a meal. We have considered the importance of meals in our lives and especially the importance of relationships with others with whom we share meals. Today we are going to focus on some meals that people shared with Jesus as described in the Gospels.

We are going to work in groups of two or three (allow time for the groups to get organized).

Together select one of the following meals to think about:
- Dinner in Matthew's house (Matthew 9.9-13)
- Feeding of the 5,000 (John 6.1-15)
- Meal at house of Simon the Pharisee (Luke 7.36-50)
- The Last Supper (Luke 22.14-20)
- Washing the disciples' feet (John 13.2-20)

Activity two: Discussing a meal with Jesus
1. In the groups of two or three look at the account of the meal in the scripture and find answers to three questions:
- What do you think was the reason for the meal?
- Who were the participants in the meal? Why do you think they were present?
- What were Jesus' words and actions?

If there are non-readers then a reader could read aloud the passage and the questions, and then all discuss together the answers.

2. People from one group join with another group who are focusing on the same meal. In this larger group discuss two more questions. These questions do not have specific, right answers, but people can express their own ideas and feelings.
- What do you think Jesus was trying to communicate through his actions and words at the meal?
- If you had been a participant at the meal what thoughts or feelings might you have had?

Activity three: Comparing the meals
1. The whole group will now be restructured into groups of five people. Each person represents a different one of the five meals that were studied. There will probably not be an equal distribution of people and meals so don't worry if the meals are not all represented or if one group has two people representing one meal.
2. In these groups of five, people can discuss one or the other of two

questions. They should respond to the questions in the first-person as if they had been one of the participants in the meal. This is a little like role playing and helps people really identify with the subject of their study.

○ What was your impression of Jesus as a result of sharing the meal with him?

○ What did you learn about yourself through this encounter with Jesus at the meal?

Activity four: Creativity and celebration

1. Respond to the study and role play of the meals with Jesus by spending some time creating some visuals, poems, litanies or other resources that would be used as a part of a brief celebration.

○ Illustrate the song "Let us break bread together" with slides.

Each could focus on one line of the song and create one or two slides. (See page 59 for instructions regarding slide making.)

○ Use poetry forms to create some poems that emphasize meals with Jesus. (See pages 78 and 79 for sample poetry forms.)

○ Prepare a litany with a series of affirmations and a corporate response that summarizes some of the ideas and feelings connected to meals with Jesus.

○ Some simple food could be available and a small group could prepare it to share with the rest of the group. The food could include:

bread	dates	raisins
grape juice	grapes	figs
melon	bananas	nuts

2. The time of celebration could follow this order:

a. Share poems

b. Litany

c. Share food

d. Sing song "Let us break bread together", and show slides

Third session – Holy Communion

Churches and groups of people from many liturgical traditions will be using these session plans. Therefore, we do not intend to present a particular theology of the Communion service but rather to provide an outline of a process that will enable leaders to present whatever theology is appropriate to the particular church.

Even if the younger people in your intergenerational group are not able to participate in the Holy Communion they are probably interested or curious about what happens and what the symbols and actions mean.

Activity one: Review the account of the Last Supper

The people who focused on the Luke passage about the Last Supper in the previous session could lead the whole group in a review of that event. The questions that were explored will provide a good outline for the review.

○ What was the reason for the meal?
○ Who were the participants?
○ What were Jesus' words and actions?
○ What do you think Jesus was trying to communicate through his actions and words?
○ If you had been a participant at the meal what thoughts or feelings might you have had?

The leader could provide some help by conducting more of an interview rather than having the people make a report.

Activity two: Celebrating the Lord's Supper in our church

The purpose of this activity is to acquaint everyone with the way Communion is celebrated in their church. These are two possibilities:

○ Invite the minister or priest to attend the class session to share with the group the what, why, and how of Holy Communion in this church.

○ If time and circumstances permit, it would be a good experience for the group to meet with the minister or priest at the communion table or altar in the sanctuary. The minister or priest could show some of the articles used in communion and explain the actions and words of the service.

During this part of the session the leader or some other people could represent the group by asking the minister or priest questions. This would be like conducting an interview.

Activity three: Additional information

This activity is optional depending on the amount of time spent and information given during the previous activity. It may be helpful to have available a variety of resources which could be used by the participants to explore further the sacrament of Holy Communion. A filmstrip, a short 16 mm film, some books with children's stories, some other resource books and an informed resource person would all be appropriate, possible resources.

Activity four: Responding creatively

There are several possible ways in which people could respond creatively to their learning about Holy Communion:

○ Make a set of slides or posters that present some of the symbols associated with Communion.

○ Create one or more banners that could be used as part of a processional and to display in the church during a celebration of Holy Communion.

○ If it is possible to have a Communion service with the whole group of generations learning together then it may be a good experience for a small group to work with the minister or priest to plan the service.

○ Some children, youth, and adults in the group may have an interest and talent in music where in a small group they could write a brief song. Or, they could practise together the singing or playing of a song that is appropriate for Holy Communion that could be shared with the congregation.

O Another group may find satisfaction in baking bread together. This bread could be part of a meal with the group or perhaps even used as a part of the celebration of Holy Communion.

Fourth session – Sharing bread with the hungry

Introduction

This whole session will be just an introduction to the problem of world hunger.

Activity one: When have you been hungry?

People could talk together in small groups responding to one or more of the following questions:

O When have you been hungry?

O What feelings or thoughts did you have when you were hungry?

O In what ways are your experiences of hunger similar or dissimilar to the experiences of people who are hungry every day of their lives?

O Describe some things you know about the problem of world hunger.

Activity two: Getting the facts

If there is a hunger task force in the church or in the community it is possible that they already have done some research and have a lot of facts about the problems of hunger in your own community, nation and the world.

There are several ways that this information could be presented.

O Several informed resource people could meet with small groups of various ages or interests to explore some of the facts of the problem.

O Interest centres could be arranged for people in the group to focus on one centre or circulate among several centres.

O A representative from an organization such as Tear Fund, Oxfam, Christian Aid could be invited to visit the group to share information, a film, and suggestions of what the group and the church can do to respond to the problem of world hunger.

Activity three: Deciding to act

The leader can guide the group in a process of brainstorming, categorizing, and selecting specific actions.

1. Ask the whole group together, or small groups, to brainstorm all the possible actions the individuals in the group and the group itself could make in response to hungry people.

2. Every suggestion is accepted. Write all the suggestions down on newsprint or an overhead transparency so that they will be visible to the group. Look at the total list and put them in several categories. Identify the categories by a descriptive title.

3. Select the ten actions that seem to be most possible and most effective in relation to the group and the church.

4. Everyone can rank the ten actions in order of priority from most effective and possible to least effective and possible.

5. When the group has identified two or three top priority actions that most people can agree to then perhaps a task group should be formed to develop a strategy in order to help the group implement its top-priority actions.

Activity four: Concluding discussion and prayer

A discussion to conclude the session could be focused on a question such as:

○ In the Gospel of John, Jesus said, ''I am the bread of life. He who comes to me will never be hungry'' (John 6.35). How should we interpret this saying of Jesus in the light of our experiences in the last few weeks and especially this week?

It is not intended that the discussion be long and involved but rather just a way of summarizing the focus on meals and hunger.

The session could be ended with a prayer in which members of the group are encouraged to participate by expressing their own thoughts, feelings and concerns.

A note to the leader

As the leader begins planning for this unit it would be wise to ask the following questions:

○ What experience of the world do the students have?

○ What understanding or experiences do the students have of hunger?

○ Are there concrete experiences that can be provided in class to bring alive the concepts of ''world'' and ''hunger'' alive?

Most children do not begin to have a ''world view'' until they are 7 or 8. Even though TV has made children more aware of a larger world and more familiar with names of countries they still find it difficult to understand distance or geography. Their world is still very much centred in the family, church, and community where they live. The leader of this unit would be wise to be sensitive to the conceptual development of the children in the group. It would be a good idea to check with their schools to see what concepts the children have of the ''world'' at various age levels.

As we looked over what we had written for this unit, we noticed that there was a heavy emphasis on discussion and sharing of ideas. In order to have a discussion people have to have information or experiences to share. If children are to be able to enter into discussions they must be provided with the opportunities in class to gather that information and to have experiences. This is especially important in this unit because children may not have had experiences outside of class in which to gather information. Our hope is that the leader will plan a wide variety of activities that will involve all students in the gathering of information that they in turn can share and that will stimulate thinking and action.

Unit 7: Celebrating Advent and Christmas

A. Introduction

Advent and Christmas provide a natural time for involving families and other people from several generations in common learning and celebrating experiences. Many churches have planned for special activities during this season which include:

○ A special intergenerational class for four weeks.
○ An all day Advent workshop for the whole church family.
○ One or more family night fellowship gatherings at the church.
○ Four Sunday night church family celebrations.

B. Unit objectives

As a result of participating in the activities included in this unit people will be enabled to:

○ State in their own words something about the importance of gifts and giving.
○ Distinguish between tangible and intangible gifts.
○ Identify some family, church, and cultural traditions related to Advent and Christmas.
○ Define in their own words the meaning and importance of the concept of "Messiah" for Jesus' day and our day.
○ Express in creative ways their interpretations of gifts, giving, traditions, Messiah, and the story of Jesus' birth.

C. Materials needed

The following materials will be needed for the whole unit. In addition there will be other, special materials needed for each session which will be described in connection with the outline of each session.

○ *Good News Bibles*
○ Paper and pencils
○ Reference books, story books, hymn books
○ Record player, filmstrip projector, movie projector, screen
○ Newsprint and felt pens

D. Sequence of sessions and activities

First session – Advent traditions

Objectives

At the end of the session people should be able to:

○ Explain several symbols that relate to Advent.
○ Identify some important family, church, or cultural traditions.
○ State in their own words the meaning of Advent as a season of the Christian year.

Materials needed

Materials for making advent wreaths and banners.

Activity one: What does the word "tradition" mean?
The leader can guide the group in a brief introduction and discussion of the concept of tradition.
○ What do you think of when you hear the word "tradition"?
○ What are some examples of traditions?
○ Why do you think traditions are important?
○ What are some traditions your family has in the way you celebrate birthdays?

Activity two: Family traditions
In family groups ask each member of the family to tell the whole group about one or more traditions that are related to the ways the family prepares for and celebrates Christmas. If there are single people in the group, younger or older, get all those people to meet together in one group to discuss traditions they remember in their families.

Each family or small group selects one or two special traditions they would like to share with the whole group.

Be sure to allow enough time for each family or small group to share their tradition with the larger group.

Activity three: The tradition of Advent
The leader can take a few minutes to make a brief presentation that will summarize some of the origins, symbols, and traditions associated with Advent. The presentation will be more effective if the leader can prepare beforehand some visuals in the form of charts, key words, posters, symbols associated with Advent, etc.

The conclusion of the presentation should focus on the symbol and traditions represented by the Advent Wreath. If some families are already familiar with Advent celebrations and use the Advent Wreath in their family then they could be encouraged to share some of their own experiences.

Activity four: Make Advent wreaths and/or banners
There should be enough materials provided for each family to make its own Advent wreath.
○ Cardboard or polystyrene circle for base of the wreath
○ Cut evergreens to form the wreath
○ Fine wire or black thread to attach evergreens to base
○ Four purple candles and a larger white candle as the Christ Candle to be lit on Christmas Eve.

All or some members of each family or household group could work together creating an Advent wreath or a hanging wreath for the fireplace or front door.

Families who have already made their wreaths, or choose not to make one, and other people could work to create individual or family Advent banners. The banners could be made from burlap and pieces of colourful felt. The designs of the banners could include symbols, words, shapes and colours. Banners could be small or large to be hung in a prominent place in the home or in the church.

Activity five: First Sunday in Advent celebration
The leader or other members of the group could prepare a brief celebration for this first Sunday in Advent. The celebration might include:
○ An opening statement and lighting the first candle
○ An Advent hymn or carol
○ Reading from the Bible
○ Prayer
○ Another Advent hymn or carol
○ A closing litany composed of statements by the participants completing the phrase "Advent is..." Response could be: "O Lord, we pray for your coming into our lives."

Second session – Hymns and carols

Objectives
At the end of the session people should be able to:
○ Explain the origins of at least one hymn or carol and explain the meaning of the words of one verse.
○ Connect words from a hymn or carol to words of Scripture.
○ Express in a creative way an interpretation of one hymn or carol.

Materials needed
○ Hymn books
○ Bibles
○ Recordings of Christmas carols and hymns
○ Creative activity materials
○ Resource books that provide background information on Christmas carols – you will probably be able to get these from your local library or church resource centre

Activity one: Singing
This first activity can be experienced in one of several ways:
○ If possible, the whole group could gather around the church organ with the organist accompanying the group in their singing of favourite Christmas carols and hymns.
○ Everyone who plays an instrument could practise several selected carols during the week then accompany the others as they sing during this session.
○ One or more recordings of Christmas music could be used to guide the group in their singing.

The time of singing should be enjoyable. It is intended to help the group focus on some of their favourite hymns and carols. Spend about fifteen minutes on this activity.

Activity two: Select a carol to study
1. Each person or family selects one favourite Christmas carol or hymn to be the focus for the rest of the session. The carols can be selected from a list prepared by the leader or from the church hymn book or some other source.

If two or more people select the same carol then they could work together as a small group if they choose.

2. Instructions should be printed on a poster or some other visible format so that people can work at their own pace. The instructions could be as follows:

Instructions for thinking about Christmas carols

1. Select a favourite Christmas carol to be the focus of your thinking for the rest of the session.
2. Check to see if anyone else has selected the same carol. You can work together if you choose to.
3. Look in the resource books to see if you can find answers to some of these questions:
○ Who wrote the words and music?
○ When and where was the carol written?
○ Are there any interesting facts related to the circumstances in which this carol was produced?
○ What do you think is the primary message of this carol?
4. Use your Bibles and other resource books to find at least one passage of scripture that relates to the same theme as the first verse of the carol.
5. Use overhead transparencies, write-on slides or poster boards to create a visual expression of what you feel is the message of the carol.
6. The carols, scriptures and visual expressions will be shared with the whole group.

Note: For people, especially non-readers, who are not able or interested to do the research, there could be a story table, a listening centre, or some other similar activity that they would enjoy.

Activity three: Sharing Christmas carols
Each person or group can share what they have discovered and created whilst working on a carol. The procedure could be:
1. Share some interesting information.
2. Read a passage of scripture.
3. Project or show the visual expression while the whole group sings the first verse of the carol.
The singing and the session could be concluded with a brief prayer or litany.

Follow-up activity
After spending time getting familiar with several Christmas carols it is possible the group could share their experience with others in one of the following ways:
○ As a part of a family Christmas Eve service.
○ By presenting a brief programme in a hospital, or elderly person's home.
○ With another group in the church.
○ In the regular church service.

Third session – Focus on gifts and giving

Objectives
At the end of this session people should be able to:
○ Distinguish between tangible (material) and intangible (non-material) gifts.
○ Suggest some gifts they would like to give to others.
○ Illustrate in a creative way the meaning of a passage of scripture focused on giving.

Materials needed
○ Creative activity materials
○ 3″ x 5″ cards for identifying gifts
○ Pick-a-picture box

Activity one: Discuss special gifts
People in the group should be divided into small conversation groups of three or four people. Each person is to think about and share with others in the small group his or her thoughts on one or more of the following questions:
○ What is a special or favourite gift you have received?
○ When were you really surprised by a gift?
○ What is a special gift you have given to someone?
There does not need to be sharing with the larger group. The conversation in the smaller groups is sufficient by itself.

Activity two: Brainstorming about gifts
1. Each person should write down as many words that come to mind that are associated with the concepts of gifts and giving. Allow no more than two minutes.
2. Each person is to select the three most important words to express the meaning of gifts or giving.
3. On a sheet of newsprint, or on an overhead projector, write out a composite list of words. Try to collect thirty or more words.

Activity three: Bible passages focused on gifts
The transition from our words about gifts to scripture passages focused on gifts is important. Now that we have identified some of our words related to gifts, let's see what some writers in the Bible had to say about the same subject.
1. There are two ways to approach this activity:
○ Offer a list of pre-selected passages from which people or groups can choose.
○ Provide resources such as Concordances, Dictionaries, Word Books and the Index in the *Good News Bible* for people and groups to search for their own passages.

It is possible to offer both alternatives to the same group so that they will not only have the choice of selecting a scripture passage from a list, but also the option of searching for their own passage.

Some scripture passages to include could be:

a. Matthew 6.1-4   Teaching about charity
b. Matthew 7.7-12   Ask, seek, knock
c. Matthew 25.35-40   "...you do it for me..."
d. Mark 12.41-44   The widow's offering
e. Mark 14.3-9   Jesus is anointed at Bethany
f. Luke 10.25-37   Parable of the Good Samaritan
g. Luke 15.11-32   Parable of the Lost Son
h. John 3.1-21   Jesus and Nicodemus

2. After selecting a passage to focus on, people in small groups can discuss the following questions:
○ What does this passage tell us about giving?
○ What feelings can be associated with this passage?
○ What connections are there between the passage and our own ideas and feelings about gifts, giving and receiving?
3. When the small groups have had enough time (5-10 minutes) to discuss the questions, the leader can bring the whole group back together and provide some time to share what insights they have gained. The leader will need to ask some probing questions to stimulate and guide the discussion.
Note to planners: Consider the following alternatives:
If you have enough time and you judge that your group is capable of the following activity, you will find it will help them to become more specific and concrete with the intangible (non-material) aspects of giving. It is possible that this could be the last activity in the session, or it could lead to an activity of creative expression.

Activity four: Practise gift giving
Prior to the session, the leader needs to prepare a set of 3" x 5" cards with open ended statements on them. Each card would have a different statement such as:
○ "Listening feels like a gift when ..."
○ "Caring feels like a gift when ..."
○ "Forgiveness feels like a gift when ..."
○ Some other key words that could be used, followed by the phrase, " _____ feels like a gift when ...":

a. Helping   f. Sharing   k. A meal
b. A phone call   g. Friendship   l. A friend
c. A visit   h. A letter   m. Acceptance
d. Flowers   i. A compliment   n. (Add your own.)
e. An invitation   j. A photograph

1. People are asked to choose a card and to think of a personal experience or to imagine a possible experience that could be used to help complete the statement. For example: "A letter feels like a gift when I open my suitcase and find a letter Pat has written and hidden in my shirts." What we want is for people to be as specific and concrete as possible in identifying some gifts that are more intangible than a pretty, wrapped package.
2. After completing the statement on the card the next step is to share the statement with a friend of someone in the family. In pairs people can share some of their feelings about the "gift".
3. Another possible step is for each person to search in the group for another person who can identify with the "gift" that was described on the card.
4. Still another alternative is for each person to write a "gift message" that could be given to someone else in the group.

Activity five: Creative expression
People can choose one of the following ways to express creatively some of their own insights or feelings regarding gifts.
○ Write a poem. Use free verse or possibly one of the poetry forms available.
○ Select one or more photographs from the pick-a-picture box and write a brief statement or story about the photographs that says something important to you about gifts.
○ Have some puppets available. Use them to make up a story, or puppet play, that will say something about gifts.
○ Draw a picture (on transparency, paper, or poster board) that illustrates something important about gifts.
○ Make a message poster (or banner) to communicate a brief message about gifts.

When everyone has finished his or her creative expression, the closing activity should be to share the creations with each other and why each was made as it was.

Fourth session – The birth of Jesus

Objective
At the end of the session people should be able to interpret the meaning of the story of the birth of Jesus in a verbal or visual way.

Materials needed
○ A variety of books, stories and filmstrips about Jesus' birth
○ Resource books
○ A collection of teaching pictures or art prints

Introduction
This session is designed to employ four different learning centres. People can choose whichever centre interests them. Each centre requires a different level of reading and analysing skills so that leaders should be especially aware of younger readers to be sure they don't end up in the centre requiring the greatest skill. The outline for each centre is written as if the instructions are being read by the participant.

Note: It is possible that the leaders could choose the activities outlined for one centre and plan to guide the whole group through those activities. If this is done then the whole unit could be expanded by one or two additional sessions.

Centre 1
The Messiah

A. Read the following statement about the concept of "Messiah":
   In the time before Jesus, the Jews were expecting a Messiah to come to save them. The Jews had several images of what their Messiah would be like. For some people Jesus was identified as the Messiah they were expecting; for others he was the opposite of what they were expecting.
B. Write down a list of four or more questions that come to mind after reading the above statement. What questions would guide your further study of the concept of "Messiah"?
C. Use the resource books and search for answers to some of your questions.
D. Check some or all of the following passages that focus on the Jews' expectation of a Messiah.
Isaiah 9.2-7, 40.1-11 and 52.13 — 53.6; Jeremiah 31.31-34; Amos 9.11-15; Micah 5.2-4; Malachi 3.1-5
E. Work on one of the following activities:
O Write your own interpretation of how you see Jesus as a Messiah who fulfilled the expectations of people in history.
O Write a letter to a friend saying why our world needs a Messiah today and how Jesus is that Messiah.
O Create some visual symbols that would illustrate the concepts of Messiah and Jesus.

Centre 2
Comparing two stories of Jesus' birth

A. Below are ten questions. First, read the Matthew passage and write answers in column A. Then, read the Luke passage and write answers in Column B. Be sure to answer the questions only on the basis of what you read in each passage.
B. Answer as many questions as you can from each passage.

A Matthew 1.18 – 2.12	Questions	B Luke 2.1-20
1._____	In what city was Jesus born?	1._____
2._____	Where in that city was Jesus born?	2._____
3._____	Where did Mary and Joseph live?	3._____
4._____	Why did they go to Bethlehem?	4._____
5._____	What ruler is mentioned?	5._____
6._____	Is a star mentioned?	6._____
7._____	Are angels mentioned?	7._____
8._____	Who comes to Bethlehem?	8._____
9._____	What do they bring?	9._____
10._____	What "voices" of authority are quoted?	10._____

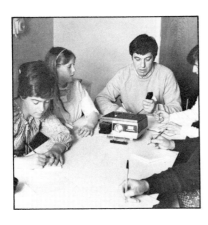

C. Look at your answers. What are the differences and similarities between the two passages? How do you account for the differences? What is the basic message that is the same in both accounts of Jesus' birth?

D. Choose one of the books or stories on the resource table or view one of the filmstrips that presents the birth of Jesus. After reading this account of Jesus' birth answer several questions:

○ Which scripture passage does this story follow?

○ Does this story combine the two scripture passages?

E. Work on one of the following activities:

○ Write a letter to one of the authors (Matthew, Luke, or the author of the other story you chose, or of the filmstrip) asking him or her questions or telling him what you think of his story about Jesus' birth.

○ Select from the collection of pictures and art prints a series of visuals that presents Jesus' birth in a creative way for you. Share your visuals with someone else telling why you selected what you did.

○ Prepare a way to tell the story of Jesus' birth in your own words. You could use pictures, figurines from a nativity set or a flannelgraph. Then tell the story to your own family, to some people in the group or in another classroom in the church.

Centre 3
Write a filmstrip script

A. Select one of the filmstrips that are available which present the story of Jesus' birth. The filmstrip "The First Christmas", available from Church Army Filmstrips can be used (Cat No. CCF 492). Use Part 1 only. It may be necessary for the leader to explain some of the frames before proceeding.

B. Review the filmstrip by looking at all the frames. You are to look at the filmstrip without the script.

C. Start with the first frame and write a brief script of one or two sentences for each frame of the filmstrip.

D. After finishing the writing go back and view the filmstrip and read your script to see if there are any corrections or changes to be made.

E. It is possible to record the script by using a portable cassette recorder.

F. Now you are ready to present your script with the filmstrip to the whole group.

Centre 4
Create slides for a script

A. Select one of the scripts from the filmstrips.

B. Read through the script so that everyone in the centre becomes familiar with it.

C. Divide the frames of the script among the people in the centre so that each one will have two or more frames to work with.

D. Use write-on slides or scratch slides, to illustrate the script for each frame. (See page 59 for slide-making directions.)

E. Put all the slides together and present the whole set of slides while reading the script that accompanies each slide.

F. Now you are ready to present your slides with the script to the whole group.

Unit 8: Celebrating Easter

A. Introduction

In this three session unit we intend not only to focus on Jesus' death and new life but on death and new life as part of the natural life-cycle.

It is important to recognize that change is a part of living and change offers opportunities for beginnings as well as endings. Families will be helped when they can think about death, change and new life at a time other than a real-life crisis. Unfortunately most families do not find these opportunities except when there is a death in the family or community and everyone is emotionally distraught. It is our hope that this unit will help people to think about birth, life, death, change, and about Jesus' death and resurrection, in order to share their growing understandings of what all this means to them personally.

When this unit was used in our church, one of the objectives was to create twelve banners that could be presented on Easter Sunday as a part of the worship service. The banners were large and beautiful. During the first hymn the students processed with the banners and placed them in stands around the walls of the sanctuary.

The number of sessions for this unit will be determined by several factors: how many people are involved, how much time for each session, whether the banners are small for family use or larger for display in the church, and whether or not you want to include some additional learning activities. If you plan to create large banners then one session will be needed for planning and designing the banners and another session will be needed to construct the banners.

B. Unit objectives

As a result of participating in these activities included in this unit people will be enabled to:

○ Describe the process of birth, change, death, and new life that happens in the life-cycle of living things in nature.

○ Compare changes in nature and in people's lives to the changes that happened to Jesus.

○ State in their own words why Easter is the most significant holy day in the church year.

○ Identify several symbols of Jesus' resurrection and explain what the symbols mean.

○ Use symbols, words, colours, and shapes to create a banner.

C. Materials needed

The materials needed for each session are listed at the beginning of the description of each session.

D. Sequence of sessions and activities

First session – Jesus died, but lives!

Materials needed:
○ Church hymn book
○ Creative activities materials
○ A filmstrip about Jesus' death and resurrection.

Activity one: Singing

Sing one or two verses from "Jesus Christ is risen today". It is helpful to have the words printed out on a chart for everyone to see. If you do not have a piano or pianist perhaps the choir could record the song for you during the weekly rehearsal and you could play the tape during the session for the group to sing to.

Focus for a moment on the word "Alleluia". What does it mean? How does it make you feel? Shout the word "Alleluia!"

Activity two: Brainstorming

Ask the participants to share all the events of Jesus' death and resurrection that they remember. Write on a blackboard, newsprint, or overhead projector all the events that are mentioned. Do not try to get everything arranged in chronological order. Accept all the events that are suggested regardless of their accuracy. (They will get straightened out later.)

Activity three: Viewing a film

To help focus on the death and resurrection of Jesus, present the filmstrip that you have decided to show. You could use "The Resurrection", which is part five of the "I Beheld His Glory" series from Church Army filmstrips (Cat No. CCF 419).

Instruct people to look for two special things while they are viewing the film.
○ Look for the actions of the disciples.
○ Look for the feelings of the disciples.

Activity four: Responding to the film
The film ends with the words, "He is risen". Ask, "Where have you heard those words before?" Sing again the first stanza of "Jesus Christ is risen today". Shout "Alleluia!"

Discuss together the actions and feelings of the disciples that were recognized while viewing the film. Also, refer to the previous list of events related to Jesus' death and resurrection. Look at the list. Circle all those that were included in the film. Add any others that were in the film but not on the list.

Activity five: Expressing feelings
People should stand and form a circle or semi-circle.

One of the leaders can guide the group's thinking and expressing of feelings while another leader serves as a recorder of their ideas. A chart on newsprint or a blackboard should be prepared with headings like those below:

Death – Crucifixion – Good Friday	New Life – Resurrection – Easter

The group will suggest words, colours, symbols, and lines to include on the chart in response to the following questions.

Exercise one: Good Friday
1. When you think of the scene of the three crosses on the hill and the stormy, dark sky at the time of Jesus' death, what words would you use to express the feelings of the scene?
(Our group suggested: dead, sadness, fear, darkness, hate)
2. Make your body into a shape that expresses *your* feelings in response to these words. (Leader can read the words slowly with time between each word for people to respond.)
3. What colours come to mind as you think about this scene?
4. What would you draw to express these feelings?
5. What symbols could represent this event in Jesus' life?

Exercise two: Easter
1. When you think of the scene of the empty tomb and Jesus appearing to Mary, what words would you use to express the feelings of the scene?
(Our group suggested: alive, joy, boldness, love, sun, hope)
2. Make your body into a shape that will express these feelings. (Leader

repeats words slowly with time between each word for people to respond.)

3. What colours come to your mind?
4. What would you draw to express these feelings?
5. What symbols would you use?

Activity six: Creating with colour

Provide paints, water colours, and chalk with paper and other necessary supplies for people to create with colour and design their interpretations of crucifixion and resurrection. People can choose one or more of the media to use for their creativity.

Be sure there is enough time to share the creative expressions with each other.

Note to leaders: Part of the purpose of the above activities is to provide opportunity for people to begin associating form, colour, and words with crucifixion and resurrection so that when they are ready to design banners they will have a wealth of ideas. The chart that one of the leaders made while the exercises were going on, recording the responses of words, symbols, lines, colours, etc., will be a valuable reference point for students when they begin their designs for the banners.

Second session – Birth, life and death

Materials needed
○ Books and stories
○ Flannelgraph
○ Paper, pencils
○ Pictures
○ Worksheets
○ Seeds, glue, construction paper
○ Items for Scavenger Hunt

Activity one: Getting started

Spend a few moments singing "Jesus Christ is risen today".

The leader can introduce the theme for the day by calling attention to the pictures, charts, and centres that are arranged around the room. Explain briefly what is meant by the words life-cycle, emphasizing the naturalness of birth, growth, change and death.

Activity two: View a filmstrip

Try to buy or borrow a filmstrip that is relevant to the theme – perhaps one about bereavement. One such filmstrip is "The Sting of Life" produced by the Bible Reading Fellowship.

There are several possible ways to use the filmstrip:

○ Show the filmstrip from beginning to end with the recorded script. Then spend some time in discussion.

○ Show the filmstrip and read the script. This allows time for reflection and

for the leader to amplify the narration for some of the frames.
○ Present the filmstrip with recorded script, work together in an exploring activity and then view the filmstrip a second time with or without sound.

Activity three: Group discussion
Discussion could begin by reflecting on the filmstrip with some questions such as:
○ How did the filmstrip make you feel?
○ What are some experiences you have had of death?
○ When you think about heaven what are your ideas and feelings?
○ What connections are there between the filmstrip and the study we made last session of Jesus' crucifixion and resurrection?
The leader can help build some of the bridges between last session and this session.

Activity Four: Responding with feelings and movement
1. Reflect on the mystery of Jesus' resurrection. Ask the students what they think happened to Jesus' body at the time of the resurrection. What form do they think he had when he appeared to the disciples after the resurrection?
2. There are many things that experience change as part of their life-cycle. List several of these things. (e.g. caterpillar, tadpole, seeds)
3. Focus on the caterpillar and butterfly. Use body movement to experience this change. Ask the group to get on the floor and make their bodies look and feel like a caterpillar. The leader may say something like the following to lead the group in the experience.

> You are long and fuzzy. You have crawled on to a big glossy beautiful green leaf. It smells so good you take a big bite out of it. You crawl off the leaf and on to a branch. Be careful of your balance. Feel the dampness of the wet branch? It is cool and a little slippery. It is time to start spinning your cocoon. Begin wrapping the silky thread around you. Bend your body to fit into the small space. It is getting dark. You feel alone, sleepy and strange. You must wait a long time for the change to take place. You feel the change happening, but do not understand what is happening or what the end result will be. Then one day you realize you feel different, you want to break out of your cocoon. Break through the wall. Stretch. Try your wings. Fly! You feel free and alive.

The leader should lead the group by taking time with the fantasy. Pause between ideas so that the students have a chance to move and feel.

Activity five: Working in interest centres
People can choose one or more of the following interest centres to work in for about thirty to forty minutes. (If you want to add an extra session to the unit you can provide opportunity to work in interest centres for another whole session.)

Centre 1   Books and stories

Gather books from the church and public libraries. Books and stories could focus on life-cycles, death, life development stages, nature, and Jesus' death and resurrection. Books should be provided for children, young people and adults.

Centre 2   Flannelgraph

Pictures of seeds, branches, flowers, fruit, etc. can be available for students to make a flannelgraph poster showing the life-cycle of plants. You may want another flannelgraph devoted to animals and people where participants can match baby and adult animals or present stages of growth of animals or people.

Centre 3   Writing centre

Have available paper, pencils and about 25-40 magazine pictures or study prints.

Instructions

Choose one of the following activities:

a. Select a picture and write a poem using poetry forms or make up your own.

b. Select a picture and write two or three sentences about the picture.

c. Select a picture and write three questions related to the picture.

d. Select several pictures and arrange them in a sequence to tell a story. Write a short story to go with the pictures.

e. Select a picture and write about what you think happened before and after this picture was taken.

Centre 4   Animals grow – some even change

What follows are two examples of worksheets that would be appropriate for this centre. You will want to adapt these and add some of your own.

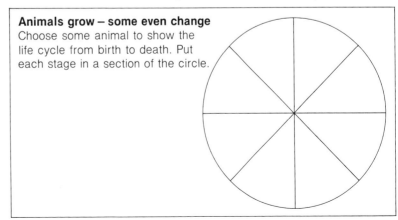

Animals grow – some even change
Choose some animal to show the life cycle from birth to death. Put each stage in a section of the circle.

Animals grow — some even change

What will each of the things below grow into? Put the name of each below the illustration. On the other line draw or write your answer showing what the thing will become.

Centre 5   Seeds

Seeds grow into many wonderful plants. Take a seed, glue it to a piece of paper, draw the root system this plant will have, and draw the plant you think the seed will become.

Centre 6   Scavenger Hunt

Prepare a table with a wide variety of items that represent living things in some stage of the life cycle. Use the following as a sample of the list of items you could include on the table to correspond with the clues for the Scavenger Hunt.

Scavenger Hunt — fill in the blanks

The answers to the following clues are found on tables and in pictures around the room. Check your answers with somebody else or a leader when you have finished.

1. Animals that live in the ocean once used a (shell) to live in.

2. A (starfish) has five legs and often is found on rocks in tide pools.

3. Find two things that produce plants. (seeds) (bulbs)

4. There are many foods that come from plants. Fill in the following blanks.

Flowers we eat (broccoli, artichokes)

Leaves we eat (lettuce, cabbage)

Roots we eat (beets, carrots, potatoes)

Seeds we eat (beans, corn)

Fruits we eat (apples, grapes, oranges)

5. I grow in a tree. I carry seeds inside me. When I open up, the seeds are free to blow in the wind or drop to the ground. I am a (pinecone).

6. I live in the ground and work to mix up the soil and make tunnels for water. I am a (worm).

7. I was once long and fuzzy and lived on the ground. I have lived in a dark place and have changed into a beautiful creature that can fly. I am a (butterfly).

8. List three creatures that are hatched from eggs. (chickens) (tortoises) (geese)

9. A caterpillar lives in a (cocoon) before it becomes a butterfly.

10. A tadpole becomes a (frog).

11. In the spring (name of animal) are born.

12. In the summer (name of food) grows.

13. In the autumn (corn etc.) ripens.

14. In the winter (trees, animals etc.) rest and go to sleep.

15. I was born from an egg. I lived in a tree. I lived in the north during the summer and the south during the winter. Now I am dead. I am a (bird).

16. I live in a shell and eat leaves and plants in your garden. I am a (snail).

Note to leader: The Scavenger Hunt will need to be adjusted to fit the items you are able to collect and have available in your room. A number of the questions have several possible answers. Make up your own Scavenger hunt.

Centre 7   Family conversations

All or some members of a family can work together in this centre. Or individuals from families could work together to share their memories, insights and feelings.

1. Create a family tree for at least three generations. Place as many names in the blanks as you can remember. (The leader can have photocopied sheets made up for people to use or families to fill in.)

```
                    _____
                          YOU
        _____  _____
              Father        Mother
_____  _____  _____  _____
Grandfather   Grandmother   Grandfather   Grandmother
```

2. One parent and one child talk about birth. They may recall memories of the birth of a sister or brother, birth of a pet, stories they have heard about their own birth.

3. Adults and children talk together about memories they have of experiences of other people in the family related to birth, changing and death.

4. Share together some ways in which you have changed, in which others have changed, or some changes you can expect to experience later in life.

Centre 8   Resurrection symbols

At Easter we celebrate the news that "Christ is risen". Jesus' coming to life after dying on the cross is called the Resurrection. Common growing things from nature have become symbols of Christ's resurrection. Their bright colours and beauty fill us with joy at Easter and remind us of the message "He lives". Discover the symbols. Follow the directions on the worksheet.

Symbols of resurrection

A symbol is an object or sign which represents something else.
   Resurrection means new life after death.
   Listed below are three objects from nature which have become common symbols at Easter. Find out why each is a symbol of resurrection. Write in your own words a sentence or two about each.

Lily   _____
                            _____
                            _____

Butterfly _____
                            _____
                            _____

Egg   _____
                            _____
                            _____

Third Session – Celebrate the resurrection

Activity
Give each group (family groups, or groups of five or six people) a large piece of paper the size that their banner is going to be.
1. Decide on a theme. (What do you want to say about Easter?)
2. Use pencils to draw on the paper all the words and symbols you wish to use, making sure you draw them the size you want for the finished product.
3. When the design is complete and satisfactory to the group, decide what colours you wish to use for each part of the banner. Write the colour on the drawings.
4. Cut out all the letters and symbols and pictures. These paper cut-outs will be your pattern pieces for cutting the felt.
5. Cut the felt pieces.
6. Use a paint brush and brush the backs of the felt pieces with white glue and place on burlap or felt backing.
7. Let the glue dry.
8. Staple top of banner to wooden crosspiece.
9. Attach long wooden support to crosspiece.

Our banners were 3′ x 6′. We used 2″ x 2″ pieces of wood to make our crosspiece and support. For stands to hold the banners in church we used large coffee tins filled with rocks with a 1″ x 3″ piece of wood placed in each can through the lid to which the standards were attached.

Illustrations:

Banner stapled to crosspiece

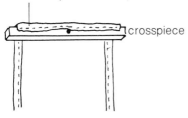

crosspiece

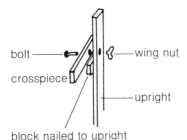

bolt — wing nut

crosspiece — upright

block nailed to upright

view from back:

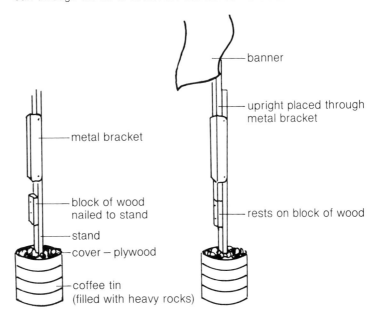

banner

upright placed through metal bracket

metal bracket

block of wood nailed to stand

stand

cover – plywood

rests on block of wood

coffee tin (filled with heavy rocks)

Unit 9: Celebrating the Gift of God's Spirit

A. Introduction

Pentecost is an important part of the church year. Pentecost was a Hebrew festival which occurred fifty days after Passover. For Christians Pentecost is remembered as the time fifty days after Jesus' death and resurrection when Jesus' disciples were gathered together and experienced the mysterious, marvellous presence of the power of God's Spirit. In a very real sense Pentecost is the Birthday of the Church.

In what follows, leaders will find a series of activities that could be used to focus on the meaning of Pentecost. The activities are not organized according to a specific number of sessions. Some churches may want to plan for three to four weeks to emphasize Pentecost and other churches may choose to have one session. If only one session is planned, maybe it could be an extended session of several hours which may include a meal.

There is a sequence to the activities as they are outlined, but people who do the planning could choose from among the activities and arrange them in whatever sequence they find appropriate.

B. Unit objectives

At the end of the unit participants should be able to:

○ Tell the story of Pentecost in their own words.

○ Identify and explain the meaning of the major symbols associated with Pentecost.

○ Suggest several reasons why Pentecost is celebrated in the church today.

○ Express in a creative way their own interpretation of the event and meaning of Pentecost.

C. Materials needed

The following items are included in one or more of the activities that are outlined on the following pages:

○ Bibles, Bible Concordances, Bible Dictionaries and other resource books.

○ Creative activities materials.

○ Materials for experiencing the wind activities.

○ Newspapers, magazines, large sheets of paper, scissors and glue.

○ Materials for planning a party.

D. Possible activities

The leaders will want to determine how many sessions and the focus for each session before selecting from the following activities.

1. Focus on the concept of ''wind'' with a discussion using questions such as:

○ What do you think of when you hear the word "wind"?
○ What experiences have you had with wind?
○ What good things are there about wind? What bad things?
○ In the Old Testament the Hebrew word for "wind" is the same word as is used for "Spirit". What questions does that raise, or what insights come to you?

2. People can use Bible Concordances to search for passages in the Old and New Testaments where wind is used to represent the presence of God's spirit.

3. Bible Dictionaries and Word Books can also be used to check on interpretations, descriptions, meanings of words such as: wind, breath, spirit, Holy Spirit, soul.

4. Enjoy some experiences with wind out of doors. Some possible activities:
○ kite flying (various sizes and shapes)
○ paper aeroplane flying (have a contest)
○ release balloons with messages
○ sail paper or model boats
○ make hand-held windmills
○ blow bubbles
○ talk against the wind, close eyes, feel the wind

5. Sing Bob Dylan's song "Blow'n in the wind". Discuss the meaning of the words as compared with some of the other experiences with wind. What is "the answer" that is "blow'n in the wind"?

6. Focus on feelings and relationships as expressed in key words like joy, sorrow, fear, hostility, forgiveness, reconciliation, love, communication and communion. Use these key words as headings on large sheets of paper or poster boards so that people can select headlines, photographs and articles from magazines and newspapers in order to create a montage of each key word.

7. Have a discussion which focuses on the montages. Some possible questions are:
○ In what ways is God's spirit present in the experiences represented by these key words?
○ What are some general impressions you get when you look at the montages?

8. Plan a Pentecost Parade. People in small groups can make banners or signs to carry. Rhythm instruments or other musical instruments could be

125

used. The parade could include singing, cheering, stunts (someone on stilts, a unicycle or other equipment), costumes or whatever else was planned. The parade could be around the neighbourhood or in the church. If your neighbours think you are crazy, remember that those who saw Jesus' friends on the day of the first Pentecost thought they were drunk.

9. Plan a Pentecost Festival that would be a celebration of the presence of God's creative spirit in the midst of his people. We celebrate God's creative spirit through our own creativity in:

- writing
- sewing
- weaving
- singing
- baking
- painting
- stitching
- constructing
- sculpting
- carving
- (or whatever else expresses our creativity)

The festival would provide an opportunity for people to share their creativity with each other. It could include a meal (picnic) or Holy Communion.

10. Listen to the reading from scripture of the account of the Pentecost experience. The scripture reading could be responded to in a variety of ways:

- writing a contemporary paraphrase
- creating a set of slides to present the event visually
- composing a simple song
- dramatizing the event with dance, movement and non-verbal expressions without a script.

11. Reread activities 1, 2 and 3 and do something similar with the concept of ''fire''.

Why do you think fire and wind are symbols that are used to represent the presence of God's spirit?

12. Experience a simulation activity which has its focus on the day after Pentecost:

What do we do now?*

We are followers of Jesus. Jesus has died but there have been experiences and reports of his renewed presence with some of his friends. We have waited in Jerusalem for seven weeks. Just yesterday, on the day of Pentecost, we were all together when we experienced a renewed power and life in a way we had never experienced before. God's Holy Spirit has blessed us with new excitement, energy and hope. Today we are all together again. We are all asking ourselves and each other "What do we do now?"

What do we do now?
There are at least six possibilities. Rank the following in the order of their priority for you. (Rank your first choice No. 1 and the last choice No. 6.)

____ I will write down some of the teachings of Jesus and important events of his life that I remember.

____ I will speak to everyone and baptize those who believe that Jesus is the Messiah. I will go to the temple, the market place, everywhere.

____ I will gather the disciples together. We need to organize ourselves, and to co-ordinate our efforts in fulfilling Jesus' instructions.

____ I will start right away healing the sick, clothing the needy, feeding the hungry and visiting the lonely.

____ I will work with others of the disciples to decide on standards for our new community to determine what others must believe and do in order to belong with us.

____ I am not ready to do anything. I will go home to think it over.

---

*Reprinted from *Using the Bible in Teaching* by Donald L. Griggs.

Students can be given the following instructions:

a. Using the worksheet that is provided, put the six strategies in the order that you think would have been right for the early church. Use whatever criteria you think is appropriate. Do this part of the exercise by yourself.

b. When students have ranked the six items individually, organize them into groups of three to five to compare their lists and to decide on a joint list for the group. If the group chooses the last one, "do nothing", then say to them, "Now that you have thought it over what will you do next?" That choice then becomes their highest strategy.

c. Each group shares with the whole group the joint list they have prepared.

d. Using your highest strategy (one of the first five, not the "do nothing" choice), spend some time looking in Acts and also the writings of Paul to find examples of ways the early Church worked out that strategy.

Some follow-up activities:

A. Obtain copies of the church budget, annual report, and monthly newsletters or whatever other material is available to see to what extent each of the five strategies is reflected in those written forms. This could provide an interesting way to evaluate the Church's ministry today.

B. Encourage each group to participate in a project that would demonstrate the values of their highest strategy. For instance:

○ "Write down the teachings" – students could write their own Gospel which could contain all that they remember about Jesus.

○ "Speak to everyone" – students could decide what they want to tell others about Jesus, then choose a place or group of people to go to.

○ "Get organized" – students could discuss together and draw up a plan of how their church ought to be organized today.

○ "Help those in need" – students could identify some places in their own community where there are people in need, and plan a way to respond to at least one of these situations.

○ "Decide on standards" – students could work out a list of standards of behaviour and belief that should be required of everyone who wants to belong to the Church and be identified as Christian.

13. Prepare for a Birthday Party for the church. People in the group will need to select which part of the party they want to be responsible for.

○ Decorate a birthday cake

○ Blow up balloons, make message cards, decorate balloons, play a game with them

○ Decorate the room

○ Prepare refreshments

○ Write a birthday prayer or litany for the church

○ Choose music to listen to, songs to sing, and a simple group dance.

3

Additional Activities, Resources and Bibliography

All the ideas and plans in the previous nine units represent just the beginning of what is possible in planning learning activities for all ages together. It is true that at the present time there is very little in the way of materials designed for intergenerational groups in the church, but there are many resources that can be adapted and used very effectively in that setting.

The nine units of session plans and activities presented in this book are intended to be used as "planning starters." They are "starters" when they:

○ start your own thinking and dreaming about the possibilities of involving generations learning together.

○ start a programme of generations learning together in your church and motivate people to want more.

○ start people considering seriously the value of several generations experiencing the same learning activities.

If you have started in yourself and in your church an interest in generations learning together, then perhaps you will find value in considering additional activities and resources.

Additional activities

Telling stories

As we plan for learning experiences in the church we find that what we are doing is "telling a story". What follows is a brief article about telling stories. Perhaps it will help to focus on ways we as leaders can stimulate interest in the great story of God's people. Stories are a natural part of our lives. We take it for granted that we will be exposed each day to at least one story. We read the newspaper, watch television, read a book or magazine, listen to neighbours tell of recent events in their lives, tell our children about ourselves and others.

As we create events in the classroom to involve students so that they can gain new insight into what it means to be a Christian, we need stories from the Bible, the bookshelf, and our own life experiences. The Bible is readily available to us, and it contains enough stories to last a lifetime. It is natural and appropriate for the teacher and the students to tell their own stories about themselves. The stories chosen from the bookshelf are often the area where teachers want help. How do you choose appropriate stories when there are so many to choose from?

Some criteria are:

Do you like the story?

For the story to have power when it is told, the person telling it needs to be involved in the story and to enjoy it.

How does the story relate to the key concepts of the session?

Sometimes we tell stories just for the fun of it, but if the story is to be included in the middle of a teaching strategy, it needs to be connected to that strategy through the concepts it relates.

Can you connect the story with scripture?

Can you interpret the story theologically? If you can see in the story truths about God, and relationships between people, you can probably connect the story with scripture.

Is the length of the story appropriate?

Consider here not only how long the attention span of your students is, but also whether you as storyteller can remember the story in its proper order. Often the longer the story the more involved it is and the more concepts it contains. How many concepts do you want?

Are the concepts in the story appropriate for the students who are listening?

This question is related to the previous one on length. In an intergenerational group you may allow more concepts than you would if teaching small children. However, the more focused your concepts, the more effective your teaching.

Does the story have descriptive words and move at a good pace?

To hold the attention of the listener the story needs action words and descriptive words. If the writer has not included these, can you as storyteller add them without changing the story? Those listening will quickly lose interest in an over-long story. Can you add descriptive words and leave out unimportant phrases to create a good pace and still maintain the essential meaning and excitement of the story? A good story captures the audience with the first two or three sentences, leads to a climax and comes to a quick ending after the climax.

A story should be fun. It should capture the interest, exercise the emotions, stretch the imagination, and provide the opportunity to "put oneself in someone else's shoes". This will help both the story teller and the listener to understand others better.

As teachers we need to make the most of the stories we present.

○ Teachers may want to start with a story to give a frame of reference, or build up to a story that may come at the end of the lesson.

○ The teacher may want to follow the story by letting the students create things to express what it meant to them, or lead the students to re-tell the story in their own words through drama.

○ The teacher can "tell" the story, present the story in a filmstrip, use a flannelgraph, simple hand puppets, a film, or slides, draw on newsprint when telling the story, etc.

There are many ways to tell the story and capture the listener when doing it.

Other programme ideas

○ A conversation hour – interesting people and what they do.
○ Arts and crafts sessions.
○ World Mission activities.
○ Stories of our families.
○ A people tour of the church – an introduction to the church and the roles people perform within it.
○ An ethnic day – finding out about different cultures.
○ A film festival.

Resources

Resources from the Bible Society

The Bible Society has many resources to help you to use the Bible in teaching. We can supply you with:
Bibles, New Testaments, Portions, scriptures on cassette and many other things.

Write for a catalogue containing details of all our materials to:
The Development Consultant
Bible Society
146 Queen Victoria Street
LONDON EC4V 4BX

Resources from other agencies

Filmstrips, cassettes, slide productions and records are also available from:

Church Army Audio-Visual Resources
Church Army Headquarters
Independents Road
Blackheath
LONDON SE3 9LG

Bible Reading Fellowship
St. Michael's House
2 Elizabeth Street
London SW1W 9RQ

National Christian Education Council
Robert Denholm House
Nutfield
Redhill
Surrey RH1 4HW

Falcon Audio Visual Aids
Falcon Court
32 Fleet Street
London EC4Y 1DB

Concordia Films
Viking Way
Bar Hill Village
Cambridge CB3 8EL

Sound and Vision Unit
Scripture Union House
130 City Road
London EC1V 2NJ

Lion Publishing
Icknield Way
Tring
Herts HP23 4LE

Mayhew McCrimmon Ltd
10-12 High Street
Great Wakering
Essex SS3 0EQ

Write to them for details.

"Write-on Film" and "Ektagraphic" pre-mounted slides are produced by Kodak Ltd, and are available from Opsis, 134 London Road, Southborough, Tonbridge, Kent.

There are very few materials available in this country specifically for intergenerational learning. However, you might get some useful ideas by writing to the following people in the United States for information, catalogues and materials.

Family Clusters, Inc
PO Box 18074
Rochester, NY 14618

Mushroom Family
PO Box 12572
Pittsburgh, PA 15241

Dr George E Koehler,
PO Box 840
Nashville, TN 37202

(Of particular interest is Dr Koehler's book "Learning Together – A Guide for Intergenerational Education in the Church", published in 1976 by Discipleship Resources, The United Methodist Church.)

Bibliography
Here are some useful books for use by leaders and students involved in Christian Education.

Bible concordances and encyclopaedias

Cruden's Complete Concordance: Lutterworth Press
The Bible Reader's Encyclopaedia and Concordance: Collins
Young's Analytical Concordance: Lutterworth Press
RSV Handy Concordance: Pickering and Inglis
The Lion Encyclopedia of the Bible: Lion Publishing
Analytical Concordance to the RSV of the New Testament by Morrison: Westminster
Nelson's Complete Concordance to the RSV: Nelson
Modern Concordance to the New Testament: Darton, Longman & Todd.

Bible dictionaries

Concise Dictionary of the Bible: Lutterworth Press
Black's Bible Dictionary: A & C Black.
The New Bible Dictionary: IVP
Vine's Expository Dictionary: Oliphants
Dictionary of Bible People/Words/Times: Scripture Union
Revell's Dictionary of Bible People: Revell

Bible commentaries

The New Bible Commentary (Revised) by Guthrie, Motyer, Stibbs and Wiseman: IVP
A Bible Commentary for Today by Howley, Bruce and Ellison: Pickering and Inglis
Tyndale Commentaries (single volumes on individual books): IVP
Black's New Testament Commentaries (individual books): A & C Black, London
Cambridge Bible Commentary (individual books): Cambridge University Press
The New Century Bible (individual books)
SCM Pelican Commentaries (individual books): Pelican Books
The Good News according to Mark by E.Schweizer: SPCK
Peake's Commentary (one volume): Nelson

For background reading

The Living World of the Old Testament by B.W. Anderson: Longman
Introducing the New Testament by A.M. Hunter: SCM Press
A New Testament History by Floyd V. Filson: SCM Press
Mark – Evangelist and Theologian by R.P. Martin: Paternoster
Luke – Historian and Theologian by I. H. Marshall: Paternoster
The Lion Handbook to the Bible: Lion Publishing
The History of Christianity: Lion Publishing
Lion Photo-Guides to the Old and New Testaments: Lion Publishing
Paul by John Drane: Lion Publishing
Jesus by John Drane: Lion Publishing
Concise Bible Atlas: Paternoster Press
New Testament Introduction by Guthrie: IVP
Understanding the New Testament Series (separate volumes on individual books): Scripture Union
The Good News in... Series (separate volumes on individual books): Fontana